Genius of the Tarot

Vincent Pitisci

D1730021

ISBN: 1480049859
ISBN-13: 9781480049857
Library of Congress Control Number: 2012918801
CreateSpace Independent Publishing Platform
North Charleston, South Carolina

Dedication

To my father, John. You've never left my side.
Proudly your son, Vincent

I would also like to acknowledge my life companion and friend,
Lynda Spino.
Thank you for adding to the quality of my life in such special ways.
Thank you for a loyal and wonderful partnership.

I thank my family for their encouragement and support not only in the
making of this book, but for many aspects of my life.
Thank you for sharing my inspiration and joys this project has given me.

Contents

ACKNOWLEDGMENTS

I would like to thank the many authors who's work over the years has help guide me along in making this book possible. Eden Gray, *A Complete Guide To The Tarot*. Stuart R. Kaplan for his many works on the Tarot, *Tarot Classic, Tarot Cards For Fun And Fortune Telling*, and *Encyclopedia of the Tarot*. Mary K. Greer, *Tarot for Your Self, Tarot Mirrors, Tarot Constellations*.
 You have all been important in my knowledge and understanding of the Tarot.

I would also like to thank Michael Michalko, *Thinkertoys, a handbook of creative-thinking techniques* and *Cracking Creativity,–The Secrets of Creative Genius*. It was your books that showed me the parallels of mind mapping and card reading, inspiring me to write *Genius of the Tarot*.

I would like to thank David Keirsey, *Please Understand Me* and *Please Understand Me II*. Your work has shown me the parallels between the four basic personality types and the four suits of the Tarot cards.

I would also like to thank Robert Hughes, *The Fatal Shore*. Your work has painted a detailed picture of life in the eighteenth century.

I would like to thank Wilhelm Fraenger, *BOSCH*. For your detailed insight on this mysterious artist and his work.

Lastly I would like to thank all who have written about the Tarot. Whether for self guidance or for divination. Thank you for sharing your own unique perceptions and insight with your books. I share your interest and enthusiasm.

PREFACE

Confessions of a Card Reader

I started reading the Tarot in 1969. Yes, I've been reading cards longer than most of you have been alive. But it wasn't until 1992 that I began to read on a professional basis. At first it was just occasional work. But by 1999, it had steadily grown into a full-time career. I've been throwing card spreads ever since.

I've done parties, psychic hot lines, carnivals, fairs, and of course a steady client base of private sessions. I've been a house reader for many boutiques, coffee houses, and lounges all over Chicago; traveled all over Illinois and into Wisconsin selling nothing but the seventy-eight pasteboards spread out for strangers looking for advice on future challenges or concerns. I've worked fairs with many others in the craft—some good, some bad, some downright evil—but for the most part just a wonderful experience. I've read for celebrities, congressmen, circuit court judges, and anyone else you can imagine.

I've sat in hot, sunny fairgrounds drinking coffee on slow afternoons waiting for seekers of the future. But I've also seen lines of people at midnight waiting for a reading with me while feeling so exhausted, I didn't think I could turn over another card.

My cards have seen cheap motels, 24/7 diners, lavish estates, and expensive corporate events. They've been exposed to rain; hot sun; cold windy nights; mustard; beer; loudly blaring music; private one-on-one sessions; and of course tears. My cards are not protected, wrapped in black silk or kept in a fancy box. They are exposed to the world. In other words, my cards are seasoned. They've read for the sane and the insane; the rich, and the poor. They've seen lost souls with empty eyes, but they've also seen many happy faces as well.

This book is not written based on assumptions. It's written on a history of experience. I made my living making predictions. The accuracy of my words for the future determined my success. It's as simple as that. I never had any intentions of writing a book. But as time went on I developed a very unique understanding of the cards. I felt now, it was time to share these concepts with others. When I was a young teenager, I often wondered about the authors of the Tarot books I read.

What kind of lives did they lead? Then, poof! The next thing I know, I'm sixty years old! Wow. And here I am, preparing my own book on the subject. I guess now, young adults will be picking up my book and feeling the same way I felt back then. I welcome you. And so do your new seventy-eight companions called the Tarot. I will be introducing you to each card personally as you turn these pages. I'm sure all seventy-nine of you will get along great. The cards really do start to become an old friend.

Introduction

Can we predict the future? That question cannot be answered so easily. Over time man has attempted to do so. But have we really succeeded? From primitive cave art depicting the future of a successful hunt, to the ancient Greek oracle of Delphi, to the sorcery of the Middle Ages and up to the present we still attempt to see into time's secrets. Does fate and destiny exist or do we have free will to choose our own experiences?

The Tarot has been around for over half of the last millennium and going strong as we enter the first century of this one. It doesn't seem to age. Like the alphabet, it is it's own language system. An ageless language system not to create words, but to create random perception and new ideas. It goes beyond using letters to speak. It uses symbols that can speak from our subconscious to our conscious. And it's combinations of messages can reach an almost infinite array of meanings. Seventy eight cards can say more than 26 letters of an alphabet. The Tarot speaks a visual language of symbols in a structured rational but yet intuitive way.

The cards images seem to make sense but not make sense at the same time. Images like the Hanged Man suspended upside down from one foot who seems perfectly content in his situation. Or the angel in the Temperance card senselessly pouring water from one urn to another. These types of images allow you to intuitively free-fall while still keeping a rational, logical consciousness.

The Tarot has evolved as we evolved. The Tarot speaks to us individually. It can quietly whisper within us. But it can also scream loud and clear. I have read for over forty years, doing fairs and other public events with many readers working together. I can tell you I have never seen two readers that read the same. We all see the Tarot in our own unique and wonderful way. I have even met successful, professional readers who never read a book on the Tarot at all. Everyone sees these curious cards in a different light. And they all work successfully. Even the books written on this subject all differ in some way from each other. But yet they all seem to offer something useful in their thinking and methods of application.

The Tarot can be seen from many different angles. We all see the cards from our own eyes and not through someone else's. The Tarot is a perfect system of self expression in the way we see the world and its challenges. How we go about to achieve our own personal inspirational pursuits. The Tarot speaks to us individually and uniquely in the way we each "see" our world. That's the beauty of the Tarot. It speaks all languages and sees all perceptions. The genius of this concept is it's randomness applied to our questions. The randomness of seventy eight cards placed into sections of a card spread to create intuitive ideas.

How can you associate this random card to a question? How can it modify it, change it, expand it. Make it better in some fashion? What attributes does it have that can be applied to a question? Today we call this method of finding answers for a future result mind-mapping.

The genius mind thinks this way naturally. Others simply have to learn it. If we define what is being done when doing a card reading, it would be the same definition of what is done when performing a mind-map. If a process looks at a question in sections, visually, in a pattern, attempts to find constructive answers from this visual pattern, adds random ideas to the sections of the pattern to help modify preliminary answers for a new insight or answer, and does all this for the ultimate purpose of finding a possible future result, it is a mind-map. It is also a tarot-card reading.

Mind-mapping and the creative thinking process of genius minds has only recently been recognized since the 1950's as a psychological study. Divination with Tarot cards has been recognized since the 18th century. Before that, it's origin and purpose is unknown. *Genius of the Tarot* will cover the basic traditional aspects of the cards and their use in card reading. But this book will also attempt to put a unique luminosity on card definitions and their applications in card spreads. *Genius of the Tarot* will try to free up card definitions and allow you to shift meanings to give specific answers to questions asked. It will show you traditional meanings to each card as well as intuitive ways of seeing the cards meanings. The following pages will attempt to stay out of the trap of using strict definitions for each card. The paradox of Tarot definitions is the more you define something, the more limited it becomes. The more exact it becomes. Which is exactly what we don't want in divination. It seems the more we want to know about the Tarot, the more we study definitions and exact detailed meanings. Which means we fall down that rabbit hole of confusing expressions and capabilities. So, to write specifically and use words of detail to describe meanings of what this system is capable of can become quite challenging. I've written this book showing three definitions for each card. *Traditional, Slight Shift* and *Quirky*. I've also added a Quick Reference list for you to refer to as you move through the book.

I hope you enjoy this approach as well as the rest of this books original perception of these curious cards. The last chapter shows a cards many different personalities it can have as a few of these cards come for a visit and speak their mind. With that said, *Genius of the Tarot* is certain to result in an enriching new awareness and greatly enhance your intuitive capabilities with Tarot cards. After all, that's why you bought this book. And now, I invite you to step through a looking glass to a Tarot tea party.

1. Introducing the Tarot

A Basic History

The Tarot has always been a mystery as to its origin and original purpose. It is speculated its beginning comes from early Renaissance Europe in the fifteenth century. A time of intellectual transformation and innovation. The oldest Tarot cards we have to date are mid-fifteenth-century Italian and were used for gaming such as torocchi, tarock, and others.

It wasn't until the late-eighteenth-century that the Tarot became associated with fortune-telling and the occult. Many names have been involved with the Tarot since that time. Many pages can be written about the Tarot's history. So here I am just giving some basic information about a select few individuals who I feel have stood out.

Jean-Baptiste Alliette (1738–1791)
The French occultist is considered the first professional Tarot occultist known who made his living by card divination. He went by the name *Etteilla*: Alliette spelled backwards.

Antoine de Gébelin (ca.1719–May 10, 1784)
Antoine de Gébelin was a former Protestant pastor.
In 1781 he went on to publish *Le Monde Primitif*. The book implied

that the Tarot was of Egyptian origin and revealed the mysteries of Isis and Thoth, gods of ancient Egypt. He also claimed the word tarot was Egyptian as well. He goes on to explain that *tar* was Egyptian for royal and *ro* was Egyptian for road. So it was understood that the word tarot was Egyptian for "*a royal road to wisdom*." After the Rosetta Stone was deciphered, Egyptologists found nothing in the Egyptian language to support De Gébelin's claims.

Eliphas Levi (1810–1875)
Levi was a French priest who saw a relationship of the Tarot to the Jewish Kabbalah. Among many other insights, Levi claimed the twenty-two major arcana of the Tarot symbolized the twenty-two paths in the Kabbalah's Tree of Life.

Dr. Gerard Encausse (1865–1917)
Using the pen name of *Papus*, Dr. Encausse was a French occultist and physician. He served Tsar Nicholas II and Tsarina Alexandra as physician and occult consultant. He claimed to have contact with spirits as well. Papus also felt the Tarot originated in Egypt. As a physician, he served as a doctor in a field hospital in World War One, where he died of tuberculosis. Papus wrote *Tarot of the Bohemians* in 1889. It is one of the most classic books on the Tarot still in circulation today.

Arthur Edward Waite (October 2, 1857–May 19, 1942)
Waite changed the Tarot cards in dramatic ways. He changed some of the titles of the cards that had Christian overtones such as changing the Pope card to the Hierophant and the Papess card to the High Priestess. Another change made was switching the order of the Justice card, usually number eight, with the Strength card, usually number eleven. But the biggest change was adding images to the pip cards. The illustrations are mostly of people doing something representing the meaning of the card. Waite called his deck a "rectified" Tarot deck. It is still the most popular Tarot deck to date.

Carl Gustav Jung (26 July 1875–6 June 1961)

Carl Jung was a Swiss psychologist and psychiatrist. He was the first psychoanalyst to see a significance to the Tarot's symbolism. He seems to have associated the Tarot to archetypes: fundamental types of persons or situations embedded in the collective unconscious of all human beings. In his book *Psychological Types*, he claims people are different in essential ways, and that we all are born with a natural inclination to one of the four basic psychological functions of consciousness—*thinking, feeling, sensation,* and *intuition*—and that these functions identify who we are.

The Tarot Deck

A Tarot deck is made up of two separate packs of cards. There are seventy-eight cards total. One pack consists of twenty-two cards called the Major Arcana. These cards have mysterious, dreamlike images and are considered to represent universal principles and metaphysical concepts. The second pack, called the Minor Arcana, is similar to today's playing cards. They consist of fifty-six cards and are divided into four suits. Each suit has ten numbered pip cards (ace through ten) and four court cards: King, Queen, Knight, and Page. Some time in history, the Knights were eliminated and the Pages were renamed Jacks to make up today's standard playing card deck. The term *"jack"* means an apprentice in some skill or trade. The suits were changed as well. The suits of the Tarot are Swords *(Spades)*, Cups *(Hearts)*,Wands *(Clubs)*, and Pentacles *(Diamonds)*.

Today's deck of playing cards originated from the tarot Minor Arcana and still keeps one Major Arcana card: the Fool. Today it is called the Joker. There are many different Tarot decks available today, but they all will have a total of seventy-eight cards and a major and minor grouping to them. The suits of the Minor Arcana might have different but similar titles as well; for example, Coins or Pentacles or Discs are identified as the same suit in different Tarot decks usually referred to as the suit of Pentacles.

The Tarot deck used in Genius of the Tarot is the Universal Waite Tarot Deck put out by U.S. Games Systems Inc.

2. How Tarot Works

The Tarot is used in many different ways by many different card readers. In fact, I would say that no two readers are alike in the way they perceive, define, or use the Tarot. If you purchase a number of books on the subject, you will find they all have a different perspective on the cards definitions and applications to read cards successfully. Older classical works on the Tarot such as *Tarot of the Bohemians by Papus*, 1889, tend to explain the Tarot with a direct, precise approach to be followed. Today's authors seem freer in their guidance and advice.

Certain customs and procedures such as the seeker cutting the cards with the left hand or keeping the cards protected in black silk are still used by many readers. But customary procedures such as these seem to be fading away as time goes by. Reverse meanings are still used by many readers as well, but that too seems to be drifting away from the craft.

Reverse Meanings
A reverse meaning is when a Tarot card is placed upside down instead of right-side up. This randomly happens during card readings depending on how you shuffle and handle the cards prior to laying the cards out in a card spread. From what I can see from co-workers in the field, half do and half don't use reverse meanings. Do reverse meanings give more depth to the Tarot cards? Paul Foster Case claims in his book, *The Tarot - A Key to the Wisdom of the Ages*, that if we were just to use the 22 Major Arcana, there are 1,124,727,000.777,607,680,000

different ways they can be arranged for different results. Adding the remaining 56 Minor Arcana to the mix would create a number of almost infinite proportions. Because of the many combinations the cards can make without reverse meanings I personally have never seen a need to use them. Many authors today will agree that reverse meanings aren't necessary and the quality of a reading will not be affected either way.

The Question

There are three important segments to a card reading:
1) the question itself;
2) the card layout or card spread; and
3) the cards randomly placed into each section of the layout.

The question is probably the most important part of the reading. First off, the answer to your question lies within the question itself. So if you have the option of asking your clients to look at their questions carefully and give them thought before readings, do so. They probably will be surprised at how their question changes into something more accurate. But I warn you, it's a bad business move. There's a good chance that by them looking into their own question deeply, they could find the answer and no longer need a reading. The better a question is formatted, the better the answer will be.

Genius minds naturally see the importance of a correct question. Einstein once was asked to answer a hypothetical question by a news reporter. The question asked was, "What would you do if a huge meteor was going to crash into earth in one hour and destroy the planet?" Einstein replied, "I would take fifty-five minutes to formulate the question and five minutes to solve it." Genius minds realize the importance of a proper perception to a question when looking for an answer.

You can find the answer most easily once the question is figured out completely. The question and the answer are part of the whole. So the better the question, the better the answer. If you can, have your clients spend some time thinking about their questions. They will see how much the questions will change into something a lot clearer as time goes by. And that will make the reading with you more beneficial to them.

The Card Spread

You can easily find sources showing many types of card layouts. You will come across spreads like the *Gypsy Spread*, the *Horoscope Spread*, the *Horseshoe Spread*, and too many others to go into. There are whole books written on card spreads alone. The purpose of a card spread, sometimes referred to as a card layout, is to create a map of your question. A card spread breaks your question apart into segments that can be looked at specifically. It's a visual diagram of the question. We will be calling these segments of a card spread "positions," and the meaning that each position represents will be called "position factors." In general, card spreads have a tendency to keep the position factors consistent with each reading. This forces the spreads factors to be somewhat general. These fixed, standard factors are set to be helpful to all questions in some way or another. But you do have the option to change the position factors as the questions change. Changing the position factors to things that specifically pertain to the question being asked can offer added insight into the question for a more direct solution.

The three types of cards spreads I will be covering are the *Three-Card Spread, The Four Winds* and *The Celtic Cross*.
Before we look at the card definitions, I thought it best to explain briefly how the cards are applied in each of these spreads.

Three-Card Spread

This is a popular and simple spread. It uses three position factors usually showing *past, present*, and *future*. However the positions can be easily changed to factors that specifically pertain to a question. Three cards are laid out face-up left to right. The cards can be read as a mix or individually.

The Celtic Cross

The Celtic Cross, also known as the ten-card spread, is the most popular and most widely used card spread today. There are various explanations on how the Cross is interpreted.

If you look at the little instruction booklet that came with your Tarot cards, you will probably find it has a version of the Celtic Cross somewhere in it. Depending on how it's applied, it can be a very powerful spread answering *what, why, how*, and *when* to any question or situation.

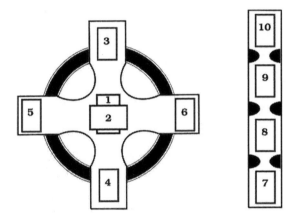

The Celtic Cross card spread is laid out in two sections.

Cards #1 through #6 comprise the cross, and cards #7 through #10 are what is called the pillar. The pillar is what the cross traditionally rests upon on actual Celtic Cross monuments found in regions of Irish, Scottish, and Welsh history.

Symbolically, the Celtic Cross represents this pattern. But for better usage and clarity in a reading, the pillar is set to the right of the cross, as shown on the previous page.

The Four-Winds Spread

The Four-Winds spread is one I came across as a teenager in the 1960s. It uses only the 22 Major Arcana cards. To be honest, I can't recall from where I came across it. I haven't seen it in print anywhere since then. So for that reason alone, I felt it would be good to share it with you. The Four-Winds spread allows you to see a question from all aspects of your consciousness: your *thoughts, emotions, spirit,* and your *physical world.* The four sections are titled North, South, East, and West. Then the numerical value of all four cards are added up to randomly add a fifth and final card for added insight. After the following chapter, all three of these spreads are covered in detail, with three example readings supplied for each.

3. Defining The Cards

Card definitions can get tricky. The more books you read on the subject, the more definitions you will find. There are many different definitions out on the Tarot by many different authors. If you are a student of the Tarot, the rich symbolism in the cards is good for study of self. Universal principles and metaphysical concepts are all in the Tarot for personal insight and growth.

But if you want to become a reader, precise definitions can limit your range of intuitive insight. Once something is defined, it becomes locked in as being something specific. From the card-readers' standpoint, the Tarot is supposed to be more fluid. That is why I've supplied a quick reference list of one-word definitions for each card. You will see that keeping the definitions general in meaning allows you to intuitively shift a card's meaning for a better answer. The cards can change to fit the occasion or situation. If you look at my definitions for Aces, you will see I have "New Concept" as the definition. This could change during a reading to be "something added to an old situation", "a second chance", "a pay raise", or something else pertaining to being new. The more you can flex a card's definition, the more range you give it. Although you will see me use the term definition in the following pages, what is really meant is *"meaning"* or *"essence"* of a card. The term "meaning" fits the Tarot's way of expression better than "definition" would. A definition limits each card to being something specific. The more you define something, the more limited it becomes. And the clearer the Tarot is defined, the more restriction you put on it.

First is shown a quick reference lists. These definitions are only one or two words and kept simple and basic. They were created by reading a number of different Tarot-book definitions for each card, then boiling them all down to a one-word definition that would be agreeable with all the books used. In other words, the card's meaning in a nutshell. One-word definitions also allow you to use word-association techniques as well. Word associations allow you to look into your own head for a card's meaning.

One-word descriptions allow you to easily use word-association methods to find new concepts or approaches to the factor position the card is placed in. And that is intuitive, and the insight you find will always be unique to your way of seeing things.

Example of word associations: Let's take a one-word definition from the Minor Arcana's Quick Reference List We will use the "Fives", and we have the word "Change" representing the definition of the "Fives". Now before you continue, stop reading and write down about 6 different meanings that come to mind from the word "Change". These can be anything that comes to mind. The term *"change of heart"* would be an example. Nothing is unacceptable—whatever pops into your head is good. On the next page are the word associations I came up with for "Change". They will probably be different than yours. Before you look at mine, write down what word-associations come to mind for "Change"

I've been reading the Tarot for over forty years. Does that make my word associations more accurate than yours? Not at all. Your word associations are just as accurate as mine. Your meaning or association with the definition of the "Fives", "Change", is just as intuitive as anyone's.

You are unique in your thinking. We all are. And we all see things from a slightly different perspective. This includes the way we see the meanings of the Tarot. I have worked with many readers over time, and I can assure you the Tarot cards are perceived differently by each individual who uses them. The meanings I have listed in this book are from my perspective, not yours. You are more than welcome to use them. But I have a feeling over time you will fine-tune them to your personal liking. That is when you are seeing the Tarot through your own eyes instead of attempting to see the Tarot through someone else's. Definitions are starting points for the cards — something to change as needed — and shouldn't be taken too rigidly. So I loosely use the term *definition* in this book.

My Word Association for Change:
• Change in the weather
• Change the channel
• Winds of change
• Changed my mind
• Spare change
• New York Stock Exchange

Told you mine would be different from yours.

Detailed Definitions

I got some good news and I got some bad news. The good news is there are no in-correct tarot definitions. The bad news is there are no correct tarot definitions.

With that said, we will first be looking at the 22 Major Arcana followed by the 56 Minor Arcana. I have put together three definitions for each card to show you how the meanings can shift and transform into something else. Lastly, I have added a few random words to associate with the card's meaning. These will be words that just come to mind from the card's definitions and description — in other words, just random thoughts from the card. Each illustration also has the Quick Reference definition along with the title of the card. It's accompanying description page has an alternative one word meaning under the title as well. This is done to show you a cards range in meaning. Try combining these two words together and you should get a vast array of meanings the card can offer. You may find my definitions wording changes slightly in some instances throughout the book. This is not a misprint. I feel memorizing definitions is not as important as understanding a card's "essence." Therefore I try to keep my definitions loose yet not confusing. This will allow you to get a feel of a card's meaning as flexible instead of a limited specific worded definition. This will give you a more personal insight as to a cards' interaction with you.

Each tarot card is capable of having many rich symbolic meanings attached to it. Another important factor is the various tarot decks available today, all having vast differences in symbolic renditions and styles. One example would be Aleister Crowley's *Thoth* tarot deck compared to the *Rider-Waite* tarot deck used in this book. Both very popular and deep Tarot decks, but different in their metaphysical concepts, symbolism, appearance and card meanings. Which means studying either of these two decks deeply would lead you in two different directions. There are as many different variables as there are Tarot decks. There are no in-correct ways to interpret the Tarot. A card's real definition can only come from one source. You. But you are more than welcome to use mine in the meantime. You will find over a period of time, that you identify the cards through your eyes regardless of the different decks you use. Whether you are using the *Tarot of Marseilles* or the *Rider-Waite* tarot deck, the meanings will remain the same regardless of the deck used. The card's image isn't as important as what it means to you personally. There is much written about specific symbolism of the Tarot cards. And this material is all wonderful to read. The most extensive work explaining the symbolic details of the cards I know of is Paul Foster Case's classic book *The Tarot - A key to the Wisdom of the Ages, copyright 1947, published by Builders of the Adytum*. Also known as B.O.T.A. The Major Arcana is closely in line with the Rider-Waite deck. Details such as the Empress wears a crown of twelve - six pointed stars representing the zodiac or the Fool wears a red feather in his hair as a symbol of aspiration and truth are explained in depth.

The details of any particular tarot deck can be fun and interesting to read about. But they tend to be inconsistent in other tarot decks. The more you focus on specifics, the more you limit yourself to only using that particular deck. This is why I prefer the one word definitions. Instead of attempting to find detail, I think it's best to find simplicity. Simplicity will allow you to see more than specifics do. It seems the more a card tells you, the less you know about it.

Over the years I have used many different Tarot decks but I always end up going back to what I started with. *The Tarot of Marseilles* or the *1 JJ Swiss Tarot* deck. Two of the most authentic Tarot decks still in circulation today. They are not very popular decks because, like playing cards, the pip cards do not have curious images on them. The Five of Swords just shows five swords like the five of Spades in a deck of playing cards. But in some respects this type of deck can stir your imagination. Sort of like reading the book instead of going and seeing the blockbuster movie. And after the movie, don't most people say "The movie wasn't as good as the book. They left out a lot."

You will come across many different definitions/interpretations to the Tarot cards. And they will all make perfect sense, which can seem to make no sense at all. But they all work. Ultimately we see what we need to see

In this chapter, the first definition heading is *Traditional*, and will be in line with most other works on the Tarot.

The second heading is titled *Slight Shift*. This is added to show you how meanings can shift from traditional definitions, giving you flexible perceptions each time you see the card. The symbolism of the Tarot can give you many angles at intuitively seeing the question asked. Think of the cards as flexible. They need to be able to stretch. The more they can flex, the wider the range of insight they can bring you. Which is why I added a third heading: *Quirky*.

Under the *Quirky* heading are examples of what extreme perceptions and associations can be seen in the cards. Some will make you laugh, but laughing is always good. The main reason for the quirky definitions is to show you the extreme possibilities the cards can have—to show you that the things that pop into your head randomly can really change a card's meaning. It will show you that anything goes in what you can see intuitively. And more importantly, everything is acceptable

As you read the *Quirky* definitions, keep in mind how Galileo discovered the pendulum clock by associating things found in a church to his quest for a way of developing an accurate time keeping device. The pendulum clock went on to become the most accurate time keeping device until the 20th century. He did this by asking himself "In what way can I associate things found in a church to keeping time accurately?" Want to know what he found? See chapter 7, *Tarot with a Twist*. I thought it best to mention that before you go on. Because after reading a few of the *Quirky* definitions you may feel I'm insane.

I'm not. (But now I must go; it's time for my medication. Nurse!)

Quick Reference List: The 22 Major Arcana

Number	Card	Meaning
0	The Fool	New Beginnings
1	The Magician	Awareness / Consciousness
2	The High Priestess	The Subconscious / Hidden
3	The Empress	Creativity
4	The Emperor	The Builder
5	The Hierophant	Spiritual Guidance
6	The Lovers	Duality / Choice
7	The Chariot	Success / Ability
8	Strength	Self-Direction / Self-Control
9	The Hermit	Inner Searching
10	The Wheel	Evolvement
11	Justice	Truth
12	The Hanged Man	Sacrifice
13	Death	Transition
14	Temperance	Inspiration
15	The Devil	False Hopes / Fears
16	The Tower	Rude Awakenings
17	The Star	Hope and Guidance
18	The Moon	Mysterious Paths
19	The Sun	Nurturing / Enlightenment
20	Judgement	Resurrection / New Awareness
21	The World	Perfect Balance / Harmony

Note: Some Tarot decks have the Strength and the Justice cards numerical value transposed. Justice still keeps its meaning of "Truth", and Strength still keeps its meaning of Self-Direction / Self-Control.

The 22 Major Arcana

The Major Arcana represent many things to many different people. For the most part, it is agreed on that they do have a deeper meaning than the Minor Arcana. A good way to approach the Majors is to think of them as universal in their essence—metaphysical in their nature. We can relate to these 22 cards in deep ways. In a card reading, we are usually looking into questions that pertain to our everyday life: love, career, and so on instead of something so deep and universal.

The Majors have the ability to go beyond those types of issues but can be related to everyday concerns all the same. Their deep meanings can be very significant in finding direction. But they can also be toned down to our worldly level when we need to find answers to everyday life challenges. Some professional readers use only the 22 Majors when doing a reading. Some readers only use the 56 Minor Arcana and keep the Majors out of the reading. But most readers will use the whole deck, Majors and Minors together, blending the meanings into something significant for the seeker. The Major Arcana have been viewed in many different ways: the Hebrew Kabbalah, Jungian archetypes, the wisdom of Egyptian gods, and much more. So, for now, if you look at these mystical Major Arcana just as having a deep, universal essence, you can proceed into deeper study in whatever way you choose to later on. Or you can just see the Tarot in your own personal way without any specific study and still do readings just fine. Again, there is no "correct" way to read Tarot cards.
 Stating there is a correct way to read the cards would imply that there is an incorrect way to read them. Although I have seen the cards read differently by everyone who I've met, they all worked fine for each individual reader.

Major Arcana
The Fool 0
~ New Beginnings ~

Major Arcana
The Fool 0
~ Believing ~

Description
A carefree traveler is seen walking off the edge of a precipice. He looks out into the clouds without concern for where he is going. He holds a staff that contains the four suits of the minor arcana. In his left hand, he holds a lily, which represents his innocence. Majestic mountains are in the background and represent the realm from which he came. The sun shines brightly on him as a little dog walks alongside.

Traditional
A new situation or idea. A carefree advancement into an unknown environment. Moving forward without all the facts. Blind trust. Step carefully as you progress. Unknown territory ahead. Surprises can be good or bad. A new beginning.

Slight Shift
No commitment needed to a situation. You are free to move on. A clear conscience allows new choices to be made. No boundaries. A total sense of freedom.

Quirky
Circus acts. The high wire. Three-ring circus. Trained animals doing tricks. What attributes do circuses have that you can associate with the question?

Random Word Associations
How do you see this card as representing a beginning?
What word associations can you make with "Trust"?

Major Arcana
The Magician 1
~ Consciousness / Awareness ~

Major Arcana
The Magician 1
~ Mastership ~

Description
A magician stands at his table ready to mystify his audience. On his table are items representing the four suits of the minor arcana. In his right hand he holds a wand which he directs skyward as he points to the ground with his left. The magician wears a red tunic with a white undergarment and the sign of infinity hovers over his head.

Traditional
Complete awareness and execution. Plans clearly made. Ability to master a goal. Carefully thought-out to a successful end. Total awareness of the situation. A centering of consciousness.
Confidence of successful execution of plans.

Slight Shift
A time to execute a planned concept. You are in a good position to convince others of your ideas. Success can be yours if planned out carefully.

Quirky
The race track. Indy 500. Imagine a checkered flag in his raised hand instead of the wand. Start your engines. The horizontal figure eight (infinity symbol) above his head looks like a racetrack. How can you associate car racing with your question?

Random Word Associations
How do you see this card as representing consciousness?
What word associations can you make with "Able"?

Major Arcana
The High Priestess 2
~ The Subconsciousness / Hidden ~

Major Arcana
The High Priestess 2
~ Mystical ~

Description
The High Priestess is seated in the Temple of Solomon between the two pillars of Boaz and Jachin. The Hebrew holy scripture of the Torah is resting in her lap. She sits in front of the veil that no one should pass. Beyond is a vast sea of knowledge. She wears a diadem of one full moon and two crescent moons, and her foot rests on another crescent moon. Her blue gown seems to flow like water.

Traditional
The mysterious and unknown. Hidden knowledge is yet to be found. Secrets and mystery. Your dreams can tell you much. Knowledge that is difficult to attain. Intuitive insight. Intuition is strong.

Slight Shift
A time be to silent. Keeping thoughts to yourself is best for now. Time for deep thought, not action. Look within for your answers.

Quirky
The B and J on the pillars remind me of a Ben and Jerry's ice cream advertisement. The founders of Ben and Jerry's ice cream were in the western comedy movie City Slickers. What attributes do cowboys and ice cream share? Cows make cream to make ice cream? How can you associate dairy products to your question?

Random Word Associations
How do you see this card as representing the subconscious?
What word associations can you make with "Hidden"?

Major Arcana
The Empress 3
~ Creativity ~

Major Arcana
The Empress 3
~ Abundance ~

Description
The Empress is resting on a plush throne that sits outside. She is surrounded by nature. A river flows between the trees, and wheat grows in the foreground. She holds a scepter and wears a crown of stars.

Traditional
Creative energy. Fertile. The nurturing power to create. Growing love. The mother. New concepts are seen clearly. New growth. Irrigation of ideas can bring abundance.

Slight Shift
A time for new ideas. Your imagination is good. You have many options for making things manifest right now. Heartfelt energy can bring new life. Something new is coming soon.

Quirky
I'm seeing the Statue of Liberty here, only she's sitting down. The scepter is her torch. How can you associate the Statue of Liberty, or other national monuments to your question?

Random Word Associations
How do you see this card as representing creativity?
What word associations can you make with "Fertile"?

Major Arcana
The Emperor 4
~ The Builder ~

Major Arcana
The Emperor 4
~ Leadership ~

Description
The Emperor, holding a scepter in his right hand, sits on a stone throne. His throne is decorated with the heads of rams. Mountains are behind him, and a river is running through the background at the bottom of the mountains. The Emperor wears armor under his red robe and has a golden crown.

Traditional
Turning concepts into reality. Manifestation. Building systems of thought. The ability to accomplish ideas and goals. All the knowledge is there. Actions to accomplish take place.
In a good position to take control.

Slight Shift
The decisions that need to be made rest in your hands. You will benefit from a successful accomplishment that is yours alone.

Quirky
This reminds me of old-fashioned photography, when you had to sit really still in the pose: the big flash of powder and the bellows camera; old tin-plate photography. How can you associate old photography with your question?

Random Word Associations
How do you see this card as representing building?
What word associations can you make with "Achieve"?

Major Arcana
The Hierophant 5
~ Spiritual Guidance ~

Major Arcana
The Hierophant 5
~ Tradition ~

Description
The Hierophant sits before two monks. At his feet lay the keys to the kingdom. His golden crown has three tiers, and he is making the Christian trinity hand-sign with his right hand while holding the papal cross scepter of the Middle Ages in his left. He sits between two gray pillars. One monk's robe has lilies; the other has roses.

Traditional
Offering counsel and guidance from the heart. Moral evaluation. Specific and true direction is here to stay. Permanent truth. Everlasting blessing.

Slight Shift
Structured counsel is given with sincere intention. Established principles will work for a better solution. Guidance from a higher position is in your environment.

Quirky
The Hierophants hand raised reminds me of a crossing guard giving signals. And the two monks have on yellow belts over their gowns like patrol boys. How can you associate crossing guards with your question?

Random Word Associations
How do you see this card as representing guidance?
What word associations can you make with "Counsel"?

Major Arcana
The Lovers 6
~ Duality / Choice ~

Major Arcana
The Lovers 6
~ Unity ~

Description

The Lovers card shows a man and woman standing naked and innocent. The image suggests the biblical Garden of Eden. Behind the woman is the tree of knowledge of good and evil; and behind the man, the tree of life. The angel Raphael looks down on them from above.

Traditional

New awareness from the heart to come. Choice. A realization of opposite vibrations. Opposite energies come together as one. Deeply felt love for another. A perfect union.

Slight Shift

Move forward with no commitments. Trusting in the heart for a bright outcome. Total openness and sincerity will work best. A successful interaction from both sides. A happy realization from the heart.

Quirky

This card reminds me of a tanning salon. The angel is emitting a very bright light. How can you associate tanning salons with your question?

Random Word Associations

How do you see this card as representing a duality?
What word associations can you make with "Choice"?

Major Arcana
The Chariot 7
~ Ability / Confidence ~

Major Arcana
The Chariot 7
~ Advancement ~

Description

A charioteer stands in a chariot driven by two sphinxes: one black, the other white. The charioteer wears a crown with a star in its center and holds a scepter in his right hand. The two crescents on his shoulders are Urim and Thummin from ancient Hebrew scripture. The chariot has the Sanskrit linga-yoni symbol on the shield, which could symbolize a stable abode. The winged sun symbol above is the shape the Egyptian god Horus takes when he goes into battle with Seth. A town looms in the background.

Traditional

Ability to succeed. Accomplishment if chosen. Fast action to an end of a challenge. A fast success. Confidence in action. Bold moves can be taken. A good position for advancement.

Slight Shift

Ability allows swift changes to occur successfully. A change of direction based on solid thinking. Goals remain intact.

Quirky

I see wrist bandages on his wrists instead of armor. What association can you make with wrist bandages to your question?

Random Word Associations

How do you see this card as representing an ability?
What word associations can you make with "Success"?

Major Arcana
Strength 8
~ Self Direction / Self Control ~

Major Arcana
Strength 8
~ The Enchantress ~

Description
With affectionate hands, a gentle woman comforts a lion as she gently closes its mouth. She seems to do this effortlessly and with total confidence in her actions. The lion seems docile in her grasp and responds with a look of trust. Above the woman's head is the infinity symbol. The woman wears a white robe and has a belt of roses around her waist.

Traditional
A force of inner strength. Will and determination. Strength coming from your higher self. Doing what's best for you. Your inner strength will advance your quest.

Slight Shift
Free will to do what others thought impossible. Surprising progress on your goal brought on by perseverance. The Enchantress will succeed.

Quirky
This reminds me of pet supplies, doggie treats, food shaped like a bone, walking the dog. How can you associate pet supplies with your question?

Random Word Associations
How do you see this card as representing strength?
What word associations can you make with "Power"?

Major Arcana
The Hermit 9
~ Inner Searching ~

Major Arcana
The Hermit 9
~ Exile ~

Description
In a gray hooded robe, a man with a long beard stands on a cold mountaintop and looks down below. In his left hand he holds a staff. In his right hand he holds a lantern with a glowing star inside it.

Traditional
Inner searching. Soul searching. A time to look within for answers. Knowledge from your higher self. Awareness from within. Knowledge coming from a higher source. The ability to shed light on the subject.

Slight Shift
Your quest is done alone. No one can travel this path but you. Solitude and inner thoughts will find the right answers. Knowledge will come from an unknown source.

Quirky
The way he holds that lantern reminds me of a lawn jockey yard decoration. How can you associate yard decorations with your question?

Random Word Associations
How do you see this card as representing an inner search?
What word associations can you make with "Light"?

Major Arcana
The Wheel 10
~ Evolvement ~

Major Arcana
The Wheel 10
~ Fortune ~

Description
A sphinx holding a sword sits atop a wheel. The jackal-headed Egyptian god Anubis is rising on the right of the wheel, and the serpent of the cosmos is descending on the left. In the four corners of the card are the four fixed signs of the zodiac: Taurus, Leo, Scorpio, and Aquarius. They are studying the principles of the universe. The word Tora is written on the wheel.

Traditional
Evolution. Things will proceed with authority and knowledge of the situation. Progress through experience of trail and error. Circumstances make a shift in positions. The tables will turn.

Slight Shift
Time to take a chance. Luck is in your corner. Things are aligned in your favor. Things are in favorable motion. Lady Luck is with you.

Quirky
I see the New York Stock Exchange. Some things are rising and some things are lowering. Stockbrokers and corporations in all four corners of the earth are studying the patterns of the market. How can you associate the stock market with your question?

Random Word Associations
How do you see this card as representing evolvement?
What word associations can you make with "Spin"?

Major Arcana
Justice 11
~ Truth ~

Major Arcana
Justice 11
~ Acceptance ~

Description
A regal-looking woman representing justice sits on a throne between
two gray pillars. She holds a set of scales in her left hand, and she
holds a sword held upright in her right hand. She wears a red robe with
gold trim and a gold crown. Behind her is a purple curtain.

Traditional
True agreement. Seeing it from all sides. Compromise for the good of
all. A fair arrangement. A strong truth holds steady. Universal laws.
Facts that cannot be denied are acknowledged.

Slight Shift
Bipartisanship. Undeniable facts regarding the situation need to be
established. A need to see things for what they are. Facing the facts.
Legal action to take place.

Quirky
The scale and that big knife remind me of a butcher's market. How can
you associate the deli with your question?

Random Word Associations
How do you see this card as representing truth?
What word associations can you make with "Fairness"?

Major Arcana
The Hanged Man 12
~ Self Sacrifice ~

Major Arcana
The Hanged Man 12
~ Reversal ~

Description
A man is suspended by his right foot from a T-cross-type gallows. The wood of the T-cross seems to still be alive with growth. The man's left leg is bent at the knee behind his right, and his hands are behind his back. A glow of yellow light surrounds his head, and he seems perfectly content with his situation.

Traditional
Sacrifice brings new awareness. Seeing things differently than others do will bring new insight. A change in position. Inaction brings new awareness. A sacrifice brings completion. An unselfish act will be recognized and praised

Slight Shift
A reversal of procedures. A difficult but necessary change. Your position on the issue is challenged. A gain from a selfless act. A state of limbo for now.

Quirky
The fact that the man is attached firmly and pointing downward makes me think of Apollo 13: in trouble, with little resources, and finally heading back to earth safely. How can you associate space travel with your question?

Random Word Associations
How do you see this card as representing sacrifice?
What word associations can you make with "Reverse"?

Major Arcana
Death 13
~ Transformation ~

Major Arcana
Death 13
~ The Physical ~

Description

Death is seen here in black armor and riding a pale horse. He holds a black flag with a white rose in the center of it. The picture shows a dead king laying under Death's horse. In front of Death, we see a kneeling young maiden who accepts Death but turns her head, having trouble facing him. We also see a child who is handing Death flowers; the child looks innocent and too young to understand what it is she faces. The only one standing is a pope who has his hands together in prayer. The pope still stands because the man dies but the title of pope will go on.

Traditional

Transformation of the situation. End of a cycle. Harvesting in ideas. New beginning. Significant change. Renewal. A necessary reaping. A loss of something or someone close to you.

Slight Shift

Old situations need to be swept away. A new look at an old issue. Act on your issue while you still can. Time will not wait. An acceptance of the inevitable.

Quirky

The shiny, black armor that Death is wearing reminds me of car wax. Looks like Death might even have some shiny chrome on that outfit. How can you associate car washes with your question?

Random Word Associations

How do you see this card as representing transformation?
What word associations can you make with "Cycles"?

Major Arcana
Temperance 14
~ Inspiration ~

Major Arcana
Temperance 14
~ Moderation ~

Description

A golden-haired angel stands at a pond with one foot in the water and the other resting on land. She pours water from one golden urn into another. The angle at which she pours defies gravity, as it is being poured almost horizontally. Lilies stand in the background, and the sun, in the shape of a crown, rises over the mountains in the distance.

Traditional

Influence from a higher source. Motivation and enthusiasm bring success. Thinking positive will open your eyes to opportunities to come. Faith in your goal. An inspiration. The ability to influence others.

Slight Shift

Easy flow of progress. Effortless transition. A path of least resistance. Inspiring energy. Good balanced approach brings achievement. An inspirational circumstance or person will become influential.

Quirky

I see a bartender here busy pouring drinks. How can you associate saloons or taverns with your question?

Random Word Associations

How do you see this card as representing inspiration?
What word associations can you make with "Flow"?

Major Arcana
The Devil 15
~ False Hopes / Fears ~

Major Arcana
The Devil 15
~ Uninspired ~

Description
A figure of half man and half beast sits on his haunches on a block of black stone. A man and woman with tails and horns are chained to a ring where the Devil sits. The Devil has horns and leatherlike wings. In his left hand he holds a torch and seems to be lighting the tail of the male figure. His right hand is held open and shows the sign of Saturn engraved on his palm.

Traditional
Distorted thinking. Deception and half truths. Things are not as they seem to be. False values. Bad decisions. A need to rethink the situation. Negative outside influences. Addiction. Confusion.

Slight Shift
Procrastination. Excuses. Be careful not to focus on false hopes. A need to move in a positive, constructive direction. Difficulty focusing on accomplishment. A lack of enthusiasm.

Quirky
I'm seeing an organ grinder with his two monkeys chained to him. The organ grinder has his little minions trained well. How can you associate organ grinders with your question?

Random Word Associations
How do you see this card as representing false hope?
What word associations can you make with "Procrastination"?

Major Arcana
The Tower 16
~ Rude Awakenings ~

Major Arcana
The Tower 16
~ Disruption ~

Description
In the night a man and woman are thrown from a tower that is being struck by a lightning bolt. A crown atop the tower is being knocked from its place, and the tower is ablaze. The tower seems to be high on a pinnacle, secluded and isolated.

Traditional
Time to prepare for the unexpected. A vulnerable position. A time to be careful and cautious. Your task still awaits you. Challenges to plans. A necessary purging. A hemorrhaging of a situation.

Slight Shift
Abrupt plans. A need to slow down and plan carefully before moving forward. An unexpected challenge could be near. Keep watch. A negative free-fall is threatening to manifest.

Quirky
I'm seeing bungee jumping here. What a nerve-racking pastime! How can you associate bungee cords with your question?

Random Word Associations
How do you see this card as representing rude awakenings?
What word associations can you make with "Surprise"?

Major Arcana
The Star 17
~ Hope / Guidance ~

Major Arcana
The Star 17
~ Insight ~

Description
A naked woman pours water on the ground and into a pond of water simultaneously. The woman has one foot resting on top of the water and does not seem to penetrate the surface. The other foot is on land. A bird perched in a nearby tree watches her. One large star hangs in the center of the sky with seven smaller stars surrounding it.

Traditional
Good direction is found. Sound gateway. A time of good news. A journey begins on a correct path. Insight. Hope is realized. Recuperation. All the pieces are coming together well. A balance of opposites are seen to work well.

Slight Shift
Look for a clear plan. The energy around you is helpful and shows answers. Others are there to help. Connecting the physical and the spiritual as one. Peaceful surroundings.

Quirky
The way the woman pours that water makes me think she's getting ready to take a bath—mixing hot and cold water to adjust the temperature to her liking. How can you associate things found in a bathroom with your question?

Random Word Associations
How do you see this card as representing guidance?
What word associations can you make with "Direction"?

Major Arcana
The Moon 18
~ Mysterious Paths ~

Major Arcana
The Moon 18
~ The Unknown ~

Description

Two dogs howl at the moon. A path from a brook goes into the card between two towers into distant mountains. A crawfish is coming out of the water in the foreground. The moon's face seems to sleep.

Traditional

Mysterious paths are ahead. All is not yet fully realized on a certain issue. Your path is correct, but more light needs to be shed before your path becomes crystal clear. Trusting intuition. Clear insight, but goal still not accomplished. More awareness will come as you move forward.

Slight Shift

More information is needed to proceed. Moving forward without direction. Cautious travel. New ground. More light needs to be shed on a dream before it can happen. Curiosity of the unknown.

Quirky

I'm seeing a nursery rhyme: "Hey diddle diddle the cat and the fiddle (crawfish just turned into a fiddler crab), / The cow jumped over the moon. / The little dog laughed to see such a sight (plural dogs, in this case) / And the dish ran away with the spoon." How can you associate nursery rhymes with your question?

Random Word Associations

How do you see this card as representing mystery?
What word associations can you make with "Pathway"?

Major Arcana
The Sun 19
~ Nurturing ~

Major Arcana
The Sun 19
~ Solace ~

Description
The sun looks down on a young child, with a flower in her hair, riding on a white horse and carrying a banner. The sun's rays alternate between straight and wavy. Sunflowers grow in the background behind a man-made wall.

Traditional
Nurturing and growth. The time is good to move forward with things. You are in a good position. Bright and happy environment. Seeing things clearly. A healthy aspect is seen clearly.
Exposure to the situation will be positive.

Slight Shift
Don't force an answer. Time is on your side. The sun will shine soon enough on your issue. Insight will come when you put yourself in a good space.

Quirky
I see pony rides for children here: ponies going around a wheel in a circle with children on their backs. What associations can you make between children's pony rides and your question?

Random Word Associations
How do you see this card as representing nurturing?
What word associations can you make with "Shine"?

Major Arcana
Judgement 20
~ New Awareness ~

Major Arcana
Judgement 20
~ Ascension ~

Description
Gabriel comes from the heavens blowing his trumpet. The dead, happy and joyous, are rising out of their coffins. The coffins seem to be floating in a body of water as the occupants are rising out of them. All seems gray in color except the angel Gabriel. On his trumpet is a banner with a cross.

Traditional
New realization. Graduating to another level in your situation. A time to rejoice is nearing. Complete understanding. An enlightened reality. A rise in your understanding and awareness.

Slight Shift
A new way of looking at old ideas is needed. Outdated information needs to be updated on your thinking. Something that has been long overdue is about to transpire.

Quirky
The angel playing his trumpet reminds me of the big-band era: Tommy Dorsey, Glenn Miller, and Louis Armstrong. What associations can you make between the big band era and your question?

Random Word Associations
How do you see this card as representing resurrection and new awareness?
What word associations can you make with "Evolve?"

Major Arcana
The World 21
~ Peace / Harmony ~

Major Arcana
The World 21
~ Excellence ~

Description
A woman dances with a baton in each hand. A purple cloth flows freely around her. She is surrounded by a wreath tied with red ribbon. In the corners of the image are the four fixed signs of the zodiac. The woman seems to dance with pride and happiness, as if her mission was completed.

Traditional
Perfect peace and harmony are at hand. You are nearing a completion to your dream come true. Abundance and joy are yours. Accomplishment. The end of a journey brings happiness.
A job well done is enjoyed by all involved. A completion.

Slight Shift
Wishes are granted. Your key to your success is your happy outlook on life. Dancing and music. Celebration will come soon for you and those close to you.

Quirky
The woman dancing clad only in a scarf reminds me of pole dancing—a strip show, erotic dance, belly dancing, hula, geisha. What association can you make between erotic dance and your question?

Random Word Associations
How do you see this card as representing harmony?
What word associations can you make with "Dance"?

Quick Reference List: The 56 Minor Arcana

Number	Card Meaning
Aces	New Concept
Twos	Choice
Threes	Creativity
Fours	Stability
Fives	Change
Sixes	Overcoming Obstacles
Sevens	Confidence / Ability
Eights	Awareness / Learning
Nines	Attainment
Tens	Completion
Pages	New Paths
Knights	Action
Queens	Patience / Understanding
Kings	Knowledge

Essence of the Four Suits:

Pentacles/*Diamonds*	The Physical
Wands/*Clubs*	The Spirit
Swords/ *Spades*	Thought
Cups/*Hearts*	Emotion

Note: I have used a common definition for all four cards of each suit. The suit definition will show you how the card is defined specifically. Example: Aces are defined as "New Concept". Therefore, the Ace of Swords would be a new concept in your thinking. The Ace of Cups would refer to a new concept in your emotions. The Five of Wands would represent a "Change" in your spirit. The Five of Swords would call attention to a "Change" in thinking—and so on.

The 56 Minor Arcana

The Minor Arcana can represent the four basic functions of consciousness: Thought (Swords), Emotion (Cups), Spirit (Wands), and the Physical (Pentacles). *Carl Jung, Isabel Myers, Kathryn Briggs* and other great thinkers of psychology have claimed that we are all born with one of these four basic functions of consciousness being our primary personality type. A good analogy of this principle is the classic tale of the *Wizard of Oz* written by *L. Frank Baum*. The four characters in the story represent the four personality types: the Scarecrow, *thought*; the Tin Man, *emotion*; the Cowardly Lion, *spirit*; and Dorothy, wanting to get back home to Kansas, the real world, *the physical*.

Where the Major Arcana represent metaphysical, universal principles, the Minor Arcana are more grounded to our life experiences in the physical plane: our everyday concerns and goals.

The pip cards, ace through ten, show the pattern of progress we each go through with basic concerns in our lives. Aces show a new concept, twos show our choices to move forward on the concept, threes show the creation of the concept and its transformation into a reality, and fours show us stabilizing the concept . Fives show the stability of the concept in jeopardy of change. Sixes show us overcoming the challenges of those changes. Sevens show us becoming more confident through this experience. Eights show us that awareness and learning can strengthen the concept. Nines show us our attainment and accomplishment, and the tens show us its completion. These things are common in all aspects of each suit: our material world, our thinking, our emotions and feelings, and our spirit and very soul. People who come to you for counsel will be in one of the ten positions on an issue. Finding out what position they're in at the present time will be helpful in understanding where they've been and where they're headed on the issue in question.

The four court cards are King, representing *knowledge*, Queen, representing *patience*, Knight, representing *action* and Page, representing *new path's*.

The Pentacles

Pentacles enjoy being interactive with others. They are community-minded and make great public servants. Approximately 40% of our US presidents were Pentacles. Pentacles are very traditional as well and will always try their best to help people close to them. They are dependable and have a yearning to belong. In relationships they believe in a conventional, loving commitment. They respects the traditional bond of love and marriage. They're devoted husbands and dedicated wives.

Family, tradition, and community are some of the things typically enjoyed by this suit. Pentacles enjoy being members of social orders, cultures, and institutions. Established institutions attract the Pentacles. This type of person enjoys being connected with others.

The suit of Pentacles can also represents the physical, material aspect of life. This suit is commonly connected to money and material gain or loss. On a deeper level, the suit of Pentacles represents the physical aspects of existence: the body, our planet, and the environment. The suit of Pentacles is the earth sign.

In Relationships: Pentacles type personalities value a secure, stable and committed relationship.

Pentacles Value - **Physical/Material Essence**

Pentacles value:
Being concerned
Trusting authority
Yearning for belonging
Seeking security
Prizing gratitude

Wands value:
Being excited
Trusting impulse
Yearning for impact
Seeking stimulation
Prizing generosity

Swords value:
Being calm
Trusting reason
Yearning for achievement
Seeking knowledge
Prizing deference

Cups value:
Being enthusiastic
Trusting intuition
Yearning for romance
Seeking identity
Prizing recognition

Oz Personification: *Dorothy*

Pentacles - Physical/Material Essence

Ace
~ New Concept ~

Pentacles - Physical/Material Essence

Ace
~ Investment ~

Description
Holding a pentacle, a hand comes out of a cloud. A groomed garden-like setting with an arched entrance is in the background. Mountains can be seen in the distance, and lilies grow in the foreground.

Traditional
A material gain that has been decided or realized. A new idea that can manifest into a reality. Pentacles would suggest this new idea could be something of a material, tangible concept. A new job or buying a new home could be associated with this card.

Slight Shift
Time to evaluate your position on a situation. Time for a new approach to an old situation. A new opportunity.

Quirky
I'm seeing a hot-air balloon in a parade down Wall Street. A time for celebration. How can you associate hot air balloons, parades, or Wall Street with your question?

Random Word Associations
How do you see this card as representing a new concept?
What word associations can you make with "Investment"?

Pentacles - Physical/Material Essence

Two
~ Choice ~

Pentacles - Physical/Material Essence

Two
~ Indecision ~

Description
A young lad wearing a tall, red hat juggles two pentacles wrapped in a cord making the figure eight. Two ships sail the wavy, high seas in the background.

Traditional
Time to makes choices between one or the other on an issue. Action toward progress can be achieved once decisions are made. A hard choice needs to be made..

Slight Shift
Timing can be a factor of your situation. I think of the man juggling the two pentacles as someone who's timing is crucial, or he may drop one of the pentacles. Getting things synchronized in your plans will keep schedules up-to-date.

Quirky
The loop around the two pentacles reminds me of a big rubber band. What association can you make with office supplies and your question?

Random Word Associations
How do you see this card as representing choice?
What word associations can you make with "Duality"?

Pentacles - Physical/Material Essence

Three
~ Creativity ~

Pentacles - Physical/Material Essence

Three
~ Possibilities ~

Description
A young architect is building a church. His peers recognize his accomplishments, and he is moving forward in his love of what he does.

Traditional
Success in accomplishing a goal. Positive results from your efforts. Material gain. Now is the time you will receive opportunity to use your talents.

Slight Shift
Being recognized for your efforts. Praise for your accomplishments. A good time to show your talents. Things are falling into place.

Quirky
I see a window washer who works for the city. What association can you make between windows and things found around windows to your question?

Random Word Associations
How do you see this card as representing creativity?
What word associations can you make with "Progress"?

Pentacles - Physical/Material Essence

Four
~ Stability ~

Pentacles - Physical/Material Essence

Four
~ Containment ~

Description
A content-looking man sits on a bench on the outskirts of a large city. He holds a pentacle with both arms and has two other pentacles under his feet. A fourth one is balanced on his crowned head.

Traditional
Security is stable. You may be too concerned about possible loses. The future looks better than you anticipate. Holding on tightly to security and things of value.

Slight Shift
A time for prudent behavior. Careful progress. Balance. Now is not the time for extreme action.

Quirky
I see a satellite-dish salesman resting after working a big city for potential clients. What association can you make between satellite dishes, cable TV and your question?

Random Word Associations
How do you see this card as representing stability?
What word associations can you make with "Balance"?

Pentacles - Physical/Material Essence

Five
~ Change ~

Pentacles - Physical/Material Essence

Five
~ Adversity ~

Description
Two unfortunate, homeless souls are walking in a cold, snowy night. They seem to be destitute and without hope. A church window with five pentacles in its design is in the background.

Traditional
Watch out for financial loss or other hardships. Prepare for the worst, but hope for the best. A time of challenge. A disruptive change of events.

Slight Shift
The darkest hour is now. Things will start improving if you continue to move forward. Signs of improving circumstances to come. Slow progress.

Quirky
The church window has no snow or ice on it. I see ice scrapers here. What association can you make between ice scrapers, or other things found in your car to your question?

Random Word Associations
How do you see this card as representing challenges?
What word associations can you make with "Change"?

Pentacles - Physical/Material Essence

Six
~ Overcoming Obstacles ~

Pentacles - Physical/Material Essence

Six
~ Compassion ~

Description
A man of comfort holding a set of scales is evenly dividing money to give to the unfortunate. Six pentacles float in the air around him, and two grateful beggars kneel before him.

Traditional
A charitable offer will be made. Someone with an understanding of the situation will help. Actions will be rewarded. Comfort is nearby. Obstacles can be relinquished.

Slight Shift
Tipping the scales in ways not status quo. Happiness in giving and receiving. You are in a good position to assist someone close to you who needs your help.

Quirky
Instead of beggars, I see pigeons. The man is feeding pigeons here. He is holding a bird feeder, not a set of scales. What association can you make between things seen in public parks and your question?

Random Word Associations
How do you see this card as representing accomplishment?
What word associations can you make with "Asset"?

Pentacles - Physical/Material Essence

Seven
~ Ability ~

Pentacles - Physical/Material Essence

Seven
~ Encouragement ~

Description

A farmer resting on his hoe contemplates his efforts. He gazes at seven pentacles growing in his crops.

Traditional

Success results from your labors. Plentiful rewards from hard work. Recognition of accomplishments. Established and secure environment. Very busy in near future.

Slight Shift

You have the resources to level the playing field in your favor. Surprising results will be positive.
Confidence in capabilities.

Quirky

I'm not seeing pentacles on the vine. I'm seeing pumpkins—pumpkins to make jack-o'-lanterns. What association can you make between things seen around Halloween and your question?

Random Word Associations

How do you see this card as representing ability?
What word associations can you make with the word "Confidence"?

Pentacles - Physical/Material Essence

Eight
~ Awareness / Learning ~

Pentacles - Physical/Material Essence

Eight
~ Achievement ~

Description
A craftsman is seated at his bench and using a hammer and awl to make a pentacle. Six more pentacles are hung vertically nearby, and one lays at his feet. A town to sell his wares is off in the distance.

Traditional
Action in material affairs. Craftsmanship and apprenticeship work well together. Employment opportunities to come. Interaction with a sense of belonging. Improving an already pleasant circumstance.

Slight Shift
Stable, creative production in what you enjoy. Your contribution will be welcomed. Unique talents and perception. Keep chipping away at the issue, and an opportunity to resolve it will present itself.

Quirky
I'm seeing the craftsman's right arm holding that hammer as the Arm & Hammer baking soda logo. What association can you make between baking soda and your question?

Random Word Associations
How do you see this card as representing awareness?
What word associations can you make with "Learning"?

Pentacles - Physical/Material Essence

Nine
~ Attainment ~

Pentacles - Physical/Material Essence

Nine
~ Wealth ~

Description
A woman stands in a vineyard or garden holding a trained falcon. Her right hand rests on six pentacles, and three more are on her left. The land surrounding her seems vast and rich with mountains off in the distance.

Traditional
Attainment and contentment are yours. Health and happiness. Comfort with peace of mind. You and others around you enjoy what you've accomplished. Tranquility in your world.

Slight Shift
Freedom of expression. Others can appreciate your good intentions. Working in harmony with those around you. A sense of security.

Quirky
I'm seeing her playing with a remote-control flying bird. She steers the toy bird with the pentacle in her right hand. What association can you make between toys and your question?

Random Word Associations
How do you see this card as representing attainment?
What word associations can you make with "Achievement"?

Pentacles - Physical/Material Essence

Ten
~ Completion ~

Pentacles - Physical/Material Essence

Ten
~ Peace ~

Description

An old, wise man sits comfortably in his estate with his family close by. Two faithful dogs are near him. Ten pentacles are floating in the air.

Traditional

Completion of a noble act will be recognized by others. Opportunity to enjoy the fruits of your labor. Reflection on accomplishments. Efforts are rewarded. A time to enjoy your success.

Slight Shift

Strength of family. Recognition of accomplishments. A sense of total understanding. Experienced and seasoned in life.

Quirky

Dogs can't resist a flying Frisbee. I'm seeing the floating pentacles as Frisbees, and the two dogs are waiting for the old guy to throw another. What association can you make between Frisbees and your question?

Random Word Associations

How do you see this card as representing completion?
What word associations can you make with "Final"?

Pentacles - Physical/Material Essence

Page
~ New Path ~

Pentacles - Physical/Material Essence

Page
~ Discovery ~

Description
A young page stands in a peaceful setting with trees and mountains in the background. He gazes at a pentacle he holds in both hands. He is wearing a bright red hat.

Traditional
New beginnings and opportunities will be realized. Fresh start. New path is taken. A choice is offered to you. Financial or material opportunity. An exciting and new option is yours for the taking.

Slight Shift
Apprenticeship. A new look at the situation will be understood. Look closely; details can tell you much.

Quirky
I'm seeing this page looking at his new hat in a hand mirror. What association can you make between mirrors and your question?

Random Word Associations
How do you see this card as representing a new path?
What word associations can you make with "Position"?

Pentacles - Physical/Material Essence

Knight
~ Action ~

Pentacles - Physical/Material Essence

Knight
~ Diligence ~

Description
A knight sits on a black steed and holds a pentacle in his right hand. In the background are freshly plowed fields that convey a sense of peace and harmony.

Traditional
Action in material gain. Accurate predictions. Positive results from positive action. A decision to move forward. Time of advancement. Necessary action should be taken.

Slight Shift
Sincere insight from a new source is welcomed. A new friend will assist you. Truth is recognized in your goal. Start proceeding on a goal, but move cautiously at first.

Quirky
This is the only knight with a black horse out of the four. The sky is yellow. The colors black and yellow remind me of bumblebees. What association can you make between bumblebees or things found in a garden to your question?

Random Word Associations
How do you see this card as representing an action?
What word associations can you make with "Movement"?

Pentacles - Physical/Material Essence

Queen
~ Patience / Understanding ~

Pentacles - Physical/Material Essence

Queen
~ Delicacy ~

Description
A queen sits on her throne in a beautiful field and looks at a single pentacle resting in her lap. In the background are blue mountains.

Traditional
Patience is a virtue of yours. Hope and positive attitude are recognized by others. Finance will grow as you carefully proceed. A woman of social status.

Slight Shift
Looking deeper than before on the situation pays off. Retracing your steps will discover things previously overlooked. Deep reflection.

Quirky
The pentacle in her lap reminds me of a laptop computer. The queen is on the Internet. What association can you make between surfing the internet and your question?

Random Word Associations
How do you see this card as representing understanding?
What word associations can you make with "Patience"?

Pentacles - Physical/Material Essence

King
~ Knowledge ~

Pentacles - Physical/Material Essence

King
~ Influence ~

Description
A king sits in a lush, walled garden. He wears a green robe embroidered with grapes. In his right hand he holds a scepter; and in his left, a single pentacle. His kingdom is seen in the background.

Traditional
A man of respect and financial security. Good working knowledge of a situation. Capable of many endeavors. Confident in success. Accomplishment through sound decisions.

Slight Shift
Overseeing the situation well. Your experience is needed by those close to you. You are the keeper to others. Graceful acceptance of a responsibility.

Quirky
I'm seeing the king wearing hunting wear here—a camouflage outfit. His throne is decorated with mounted trophies of previous hunts and his left foot rest on his most recent prize.
What association can you make between camouflage hunting sportswear and your question?

Random Word Associations
How do you see this card as representing knowledge?
What word associations can you make with "Wise"?

The Wands

The suit of Wands' personality is one of excitement. People who are Wands are risk-takers and enjoy doing things out of the ordinary. Wands are less concerned with security or a stable lifestyle than the other suits are. Wands don't like being tied down to routines. They are spontaneous in action. When involved in some artistic activity, they become intensely focused and have unending drive. Wands can electrify the moment or a group. They stand out with confidence and have impact when in their own environment. Wands can act on impulse and are quick-minded. They don't want to miss anything. They want to experience everything. But once Wands settle down, they can be very loyal mates. Wands are very passionate about life. Their intense drive makes them great accomplishers in their pursuits. If they are interested in something, they bury themselves in the project.

The suit of Wands is the fire sign. Wands also represent the spirit and inspirations of things in your life. Wands is the energy that drives the spirit onward. What inspires us.

In Relationships: Wands type personalities value a playful, exciting relationship.

Wands Value – Spirit / Inspirational Essence

Wands value:
Being excited
Trusting impulse
Yearning for impact
Seeking stimulation
Prizing generosity

Pentacles value:
Being concerned
Trusting authority
Yearning for belonging
Seeking security
Prizing gratitude

Swords value:
Being calm
Trusting reason
Yearning for achievement
Seeking knowledge
Prizing deference

Cups value:
Being enthusiastic
Trusting intuition
Yearning for romance
Seeking identity
Prizing recognition

Oz Personification: *The Lion*

The Wands - Spirit/Inspirational Essence

Ace
~ New Concept ~

The Wands - Spirit/Inspirational Essence

Ace
~ Ambition ~

Description

A hand comes out of a cloud holding a staff with sparse growth on it. In the background are mountains with some trees and a river. A castle is in the distance.

Traditional

New inspirations. New spirit for a fresh idea. Goals set with clear vision. Sound planning of a particular desire. Positive action taken from the soul. A new beginning.

Slight Shift

A new path is taken. Opportunities will come to pass. A need for inspiration. Dreams can now become a reality. Focus on finding your center. Seeing the possibilities clearly.

Quirky

The wand with the bit of growth on it looks like a bonsai tree in need of help. What association can you make between bonsai trees and your question?

Random Word Associations

How do you see this card as representing a new beginning?
What word associations can you make with "Spirit"?

The Wands - Spirit/Inspirational Essence

Two
~ Choice ~

The Wands - Spirit/Inspirational Essence

Two
~ Offering ~

Description
A man stands on a balcony overlooking a beautiful landscape of trees, mountains, and a lake. He holds a sphere that resembles the world in his right hand. His left hand holds a staff. A second staff is attached to a nearby wall.

Traditional
A sincere offer. A strong belief in your quest. Positive opportunities. Decisions are made for a possible gratifying situation. Opportunity for a goal with real purpose is near.

Slight Shift
An ally. Working as a team on a common interest. Seeing more than was seen before brings new possibilities and perception to the goal at hand. You have inspired others in your quest.

Quirky
I'm seeing a snow globe in his hand. What association can you make between snow globes or music boxes to your question?

Random Word Associations
How do you see this card as representing choice?
What word associations can you make with "Options"?

The Wands - Spirit/Inspirational Essence

Three
~ Creativity ~

The Wands - Spirit/Inspirational Essence

Three
~ Scope ~

Description

A man stands on a mountain looking down on a golden lake with sailing ships in the distance. Mountains are seen far-off. He holds a staff, and two other staffs stand nearby.

Traditional

Insight brings new possibilities. Many things are realized about a goal. New interaction on an enterprise. Realizations and awareness are put into action. Growth in perceiving your goal clearly. Answers are found.

Slight Shift

A need to focus on direction. Fine-tune your goal to achieve an end result. A time to look at long-term goals. Big decisions are in the making.

Quirky

The man standing here is a travel agent watching his three cruise ships leaving port with his clients on board. What association can you make with cruise ships or travel to your question.

Random Word Associations

How do you see this card as representing creativity?
What word associations can you make with "Awareness"?

The Wands - Spirit/Inspirational Essence

Four
~ Stability ~

The Wands - Spirit/Inspirational Essence

Four
~ Uplifting ~

Description
Four staffs are decorated as if for a festivity. Two maidens hold up
flowers in a celebrating fashion. In the background is a castle, and
more people are gathering toward it.

Traditional
Joyous times. All is working as planned. Things fall into place. Good
harmony. In a good position on an issue. Stable and dependable situation makes things enjoyable.

Slight Shift
Consistency makes things pleasant. Planning is easy for the future.
Recognition is seen by others on a successful achievement.

Quirky
This looks like a party. I'm seeing party supplies: brightly colored
paper plates, plastic cups, and paper tablecloths. What association can
you make between party supplies and your question?

Random Word Associations
How do you see this card as representing stability?
What word associations can you make with "Consistent"?

The Wands - Spirit/Inspirational Essence

Five
~ Change ~

The Wands - Spirit/Inspirational Essence

Five
~ Stimulation ~

Description
Five men seem to be fighting among themselves. All the men are dressed in different garb, suggesting clannish differences.

Traditional
A situation is challenged. Different opinions create change in circumstances. Cautious action needs to be taken. Change of heart. A difference of opinions causes polarity in dialogue.

Slight Shift
Misunderstandings need to be explained. Not a time for action. Patience is needed now. A time for diplomacy. An opportunity to settle disagreements.

Quirky
I'm seeing these men trying to put up a tent. They are having difficulty figuring out how the tent poles are to be set up. How can you associate camping equipment with your question?

Random Word Associations
How do you see this card as representing change?
What word associations can you make with "Conflict"?

The Wands - Spirit/Inspirational Essence

Six
~ Overcoming Obstacles ~

The Wands - Spirit/Inspirational Essence

Six
~ Celebration ~

Description
A victorious rider is celebrated by his peers. He carries a staff decorated with a laurel. He wears a second laurel on his head. People on foot, carrying staffs, follow him.

Traditional
Successful efforts are accomplished. Adversity is overcome. A bad situation can or has been eliminated. Success is recognized. A difficult challenge can be successfully overcome if you persevere.

Slight Shift
The time is now to face challenges. A good position to take on opposing forces takes shape. Actions give positive results. Sound judgment and strategy reap rewards.

Quirky
That white horse is looking at us like he knows something we don't. I'm seeing Mr. Ed, the talking horse here. What associations can you make between old sitcoms and your question?

Random Word Associations
How do you see this card as representing success?
What word associations can you make with "Win"?

The Wands - Spirit/Inspirational Essence

Seven
~ Confidence / Ability ~

The Wands - Spirit/Inspirational Essence

Seven
~ Sustainment ~

Description
A young man gripping a staff seems to be holding off six other staffs. He seems to be on the very edge of a cliff, preventing him from stepping backward.

Traditional
Convincing others of a viewpoint. Stressful circumstances turn for the better because of actions taken. Your ability to succeed is respected. Moving forward with spirit will win the day.

Slight Shift
Others may disagree with your perspective on an issue. Time will allow them to see your point with more clarity. Biding your time. Staying firm on a belief.

Quirky
I'm seeing the man here building a fence. What association can you make between fences and your question?

Random Word Associations
How do you see this card as representing ability?
What word associations can you make with "Debate"?

The Wands - Spirit/Inspirational Essence

Eight
~ Awareness / Learning ~

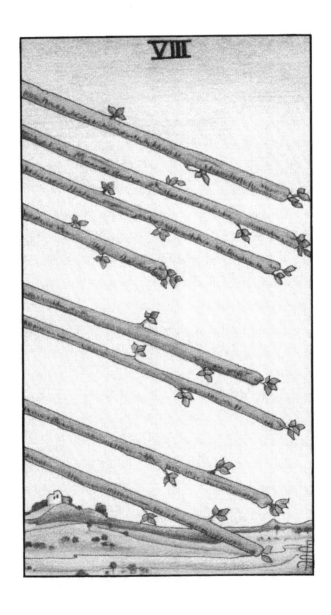

The Wands - Spirit/Inspirational Essence

Eight
~ Clarity ~

Description
Eight staffs fly through the air in the same direction. In the distance a house sits on a gentle green slope just above a river.

Traditional
Moving forward quickly with little resistance. A time to strengthen a situation by taking action to do more. Added stability to an already positive position.

Slight Shift
Swift accomplishment. Past experience pays off. Learning as you move forward. A clear and quick result. Caution on moving too quickly. Haste can make waste.

Quirky
These staffs remind me of pretzel sticks with big chunks of salt stuck to them. What association can you make with TV snacks to your question?

Random Word Associations
How do you see this card as representing awareness?
What word associations can you make with "Swift"?

The Wands - Spirit/Inspirational Essence

Nine
~ Attainment ~

The Wands - Spirit/Inspirational Essence

Nine
~ Determination ~

Description
A man stands alone wearing a bandage on his head. He holds one staff and eight other staffs are standing behind him. Mountains are in the background,

Traditional
Acquired value. A challenging accomplishment. A struggle has ended. Efforts made in a hard-fought goal have paid off. Truly tested strength still remains.

Slight Shift
Enjoy the fruits of your labor. A seasoned vet. A destination is reached. Peace of mind will come soon if you stay firm.

Quirky
I'm seeing the staffs as other people who are all on a subway. The man feels crowded as he waits for his stop. How can you associate commuting with your question?

Random Word Associations
How do you see this card as representing attainment?
What word associations can you make with "Perseverance"?

The Wands - Spirit/Inspirational Essence

Ten
~ Completion ~

The Wands - Spirit/Inspirational Essence

Ten
~ Gathered ~

Description
A man is carrying ten staffs. In the background is a house and trees.

Traditional
The end of one cycle and the beginning of another. Completion allows for a fresh start. Moving on to a higher level of a situation. A task is complete.

Slight Shift
The last in a series of events. Last piece of the puzzle. Gathering things for closure. Complete closure. Finality. All has been gathered and accounted for.

Quirky
I'm seeing a boy counting with his face buried in the bundle of staffs. His friends are going about hiding as he counts. He is playing hide and seek. What association can you make between children's games and your question?

Random Word Associations
How do you see this card as representing completion?
What word associations can you make with "Closure"?

The Wands - Spirit/Inspirational Essence

Page
~ New Paths ~

PAGE of WANDS.

The Wands - Spirit/Inspirational Essence

Page
~ Vision ~

Description
A young page stands tall and admires a staff he holds in his hands. In the background are three pyramids. He appears to be in a far-off, mysterious land.

Traditional
A new inspiration or goal. New choices. A decision is made. After the completion of the tens, the page starts a new endeavor. A new set of circumstances.

Slight Shift
New options. The choice is yours to make. Don't force an answer. It will come to you in time. Follow your spirits quest.

Quirky
I'm seeing a golf caddy holding the flagstick. How can you associate golf resorts with your question?

Random Word Associations
How do you see this card as representing new paths?
What word associations can you make with "Start"?

The Wands - Spirit/Inspirational Essence

Knight
~ Action ~

The Wands - Spirit/Inspirational Essence

Knight
~ Intensity ~

Description
Exploring a far-off land, a knight rides along on a golden steed. He carries a staff in his right hand. Three pyramids are off in the distance.

Traditional
Now is the time to act on the issue at hand. A time to make intentions known. The time for talk has already been accomplished. Following through is the best course of action.

Slight Shift
Steps need to be taken in correct order. Move with confidence in your undertakings. Your time is now. A window of opportunity will not stay open for long. The longer you wait, the slower the progress will be. Action is key.

Quirky
I'm seeing a neck brace around his neck instead of a lower portion of the helmet. What association can you make between neck braces and your question?

Random Word Associations
How do you see this card as representing action?
What word associations can you make with "Knights"?

The Wands - Spirit/Inspirational Essence

Queen
~ Patience / Understanding ~

The Wands - Spirit/Inspirational Essence

Queen
~ Respect ~

Description

Holding a flower in her left hand, a queen sits on her throne. In her right hand she holds a staff. Three pyramids are off in the distance, and a black cat sits at the queen's feet.

Traditional

A complete understanding of the situation. All the facts on the table before decisions are made. Look at all angles. Tricky choices. Great insight on the issue. A wise and caring ally.

Slight Shift

Care and compassion will get you far. Success by inaction instead of action. Lay low a while and watch to see if things change on their own.

Quirky

I'm seeing a woman who has entered a pet show with her prize cat hoping to get the Blue Ribbon. She is looking over at the judges as they are about to make their choice. What association can you make between pet shows and your question?

Random Word Associations

How do you see this card as representing patience?
What word associations can you make with "Silence"?

The Wands - Spirit/Inspirational Essence

King
~ Knowledge ~

KING of WANDS

The Wands - Spirit/Inspirational Essence

King
~ Wisdom ~

Description
A king holding a staff in his right hand sits on his throne in profile. He seems to be in deep thought. A salamander, the sign of fire, is near his feet.

Tradition
Wisdom of an experienced person. Leading the way with confidence in one's ability. Total understanding of the goal. Opinions are respected. Enthusiasm for a specific desire.

Slight Shift
More knowledge of the situation is needed. Complete understanding will get good results. Seek the advice of another with experience in this issue.

Quirky
I'm seeing a hockey player in the penalty box. The staff is a hockey stick. He's waiting anxiously with his left hand clenched in a fist to get back in the game. What association can you make between hockey equipment and your question?

Random Word Associations
How do you see this card as representing knowledge?
What word associations can you make with "Leadership"?

The Swords

The suit of Swords personality is one of deep thought. When people who are Swords have something to solve, they can focus on the issue fully. Concerning themselves with logical investigations of things, they tend to shy away from others. But this doesn't mean they don't care about others. They do. And when their focus is on someone close to them, they are very obliging. Swords enjoy thinking about possibilities and the probable outcomes they may possess. Swords act with logic. And they face challenges with a clear head. They are loyal, uncomplaining, and are not possessive. They are not easy to get close to because of their complex personality. But once you do establish a relationship with this type, they will face any challenge the relationship may have. They don't give up on it easily. They face challenge with determination and strong focus. Like all the suits, Swords can make wonderful mates.

The suit of Swords is the air sign. Swords also represent the concepts and perception of things in your life. Swords give us the ability to think challenges through.

In Relationships: Swords value relationships that are intellectually stimulating

Swords Value - **Essence of Thought**

Swords value:
Being calm
Trusting reason
Yearning for achievement
Seeking knowledge
Prizing deference

Cups value:
Being enthusiastic
Trusting intuition
Yearning for romance
Seeking identity
Prizing recognition

Wands value:
Being excited
Trusting impulse
Yearning for impact
Seeking stimulation
Prizing generosity

Pentacles value:
Being concerned
Trusting authority
Yearning for belonging
Seeking security
Prizing gratitude

Oz Personification: *The Scarecrow*

The Swords - **Essence of Thought**

Ace
~ New Concept ~

The Swords - Essence of Thought

Ace
~ Situations ~

Description

A hand holding a sword comes out of a cloud. A crown with hanging leaves hovers in the air at the end of the sword. Mountains are in the distance.

Traditional

A new idea. A better way to proceed. New direction and perception. A good understanding of what should be done. A realization based on new information.

Slight Shift

The sword going through the crown shows a breakthrough in your thinking. Rational thinking overrules emotions. Seeing all facts clearly.

Quirky

I'm seeing a fondue. The crown, with garnish added, is ready to eat. What association can you make between fondues and your question?

Random Word Associations

How do you see this card as a representing a breakthrough?
What word associations can you make with "Revelation"?

The Swords - Essence of Thought

Two
~ Choice ~

The Swords - Essence of Thought

Two
~ Balance ~

Description
A woman who is blindfolded crosses two swords on her shoulders. She is sitting on a bench with her back to a lake. A crescent moon looms over her left shoulder in the night sky.

Traditional
Hard choices to be made. Careful thought before action needs to be taken. Inaction caused by lack of knowing. More information is still needed in order to move forward. A sense of confusion.

Slight Shift
Action taken from a hunch is the only option for now. Trust your instincts. A stab in the dark. A new sense of balance.

Quirky
I'm seeing her wearing a sweatband that's hanging too low over her eyes. What association can you make between sweatbands or jogging outfits and your question?

Random Word Associations
How do you see this card as representing a choice?
What word associations can you make with "Split"?

The Swords - **Essence of Thought**

Three
~ Creativity ~

The Swords - Essence of Thought

Three
~ Threshold ~

Description
Three swords are driven into a red heart. Rain and grey clouds are in the background.

Traditional
Awareness of a sad truth. A search for options to resolve an issue of concern. An unhappy but necessary decision. A time for healing. Unhappy news from the heart. Anxiety.

Slight Shift
Unpleasant action needed to attain a happy outcome. An issue needs to be addressed. The time to make hard choices is near.

Quirky
I'm seeing the three swords as umbrellas stuck in an umbrella holder. What association can you make between umbrellas and your question?

Random Word Associations
How do you see this card as representing creativity?
What word associations can you make with "Difficult"?

The Swords - Essence of Thought

Four
~ Stability ~

The Swords - Essence of Thought

Four
~ Secure ~

Description
The effigy of a praying knight lies on his tomb in a church. Three swords are hung on the wall near a stained-glass window. A fourth sword is on the side of his tomb.

Traditional
Regroup and contemplate the situation. A clear mind will find answers. Inaction is best for now. A time to rest. Quieting the mind. Healing after a challenging time. Rest will make for a better frame of mind.

Slight Shift
Patience will bring a better perspective of the situation. A time to see things from a different viewpoint. Action is difficult at this time. A time to stop and think clearly.

Quirky
I'm seeing the funeral parlor. What things do we see in funeral parlors? Folding chairs, Styrofoam coffee cups, name plates, and flowers. What association can you make between things found in funeral parlors and your question?

Random Word Associations
How do you see this card as representing stability?
What word associations can you make with "Still"?

The Swords - **Essence of Thought**

Five
~ Change ~

The Swords - Essence of Thought

Five
~ Intervention ~

Description
A man holds three swords as two other men walk away toward a body of water. Two more swords are lying on the ground near the first man's feet. Clouds in the sky seem to hint a storm is in the air.

Traditional
Opposition is faced. Confrontation will clear the air. Action will take place soon. Differences between those close to you. A time for debate. Prepare for a threat to your current position.

Slight Shift
Clean sweep. Clearing the air of differences. A direct position on an issue is clearly understood. Hold your ground if you truly believe in your stance on the subject.

Quirky
I'm seeing the man's hair as a wacky, punk-rock hairstyle. What association can you make between things found in barber shops or hair salons and your question?

Random Word Associations
How do you see this card as representing a change?
What word associations can you make with "Attack"?

The Swords - Essence of Thought

Six
~ Overcoming Obstacles ~

The Swords - Essence of Thought

Six
~ Assurance ~

Description
A man ferries a woman and child across the water. Six swords are stuck into the bottom of the boat. The water seems more peaceful as they move forward.

Traditional
Things are improving steadily. Moving on to calmer waters. Actions taken are seeing results. Peace of mind will come soon. Today's efforts improve the situation. Plans are showing progress.

Slight Shift
Recent struggles have been overcome. Sanctuary. Harmony is restored. Tranquility after a hard loss is attained.

Quirky
The six swords remind me of the El train. The El train has gates that can't be passed until a purchased ticket is inserted before boarding. What association can you make between things found in train stations and your question?

Random Word Associations
How do you see this card as representing an accomplishment?
What word associations can you make with "Waves"?

The Swords - Essence of Thought

Seven
~ Confidence / Ability ~

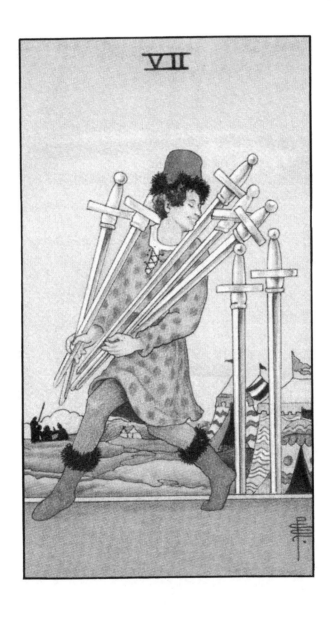

The Swords - Essence of Thought

Seven
~ Discretion ~

Description
A man steals away carrying five swords from an enemy camp. Two
other swords are stuck in the ground behind him. The enemy camp is
in the background.

Traditional
You are in a good position to act. Success because of your strong
points on the issue. Reason and good judgment. Sound action can take
place now.

Slight Shift
Improvise. Shooting from the hip. You have the talent to do things differently than usually anticipated. You have the advantage of surprise.

Quirky
I'm seeing the man planting swords in the ground as a landscaper
would, not taking them away. What association can you make between
nurseries and your question?

Random Word Associations
How do you see this card as representing confidence?
What word associations can you make with "Sneak"?

The Swords - Essence of Thought

Eight
~ Awareness / Learning ~

The Swords - Essence of Thought

Eight
~ Denial ~

Description
A woman bound and blindfolded stands in a watery wasteland. She is surrounded by eight swords. In the distance is a mountain with a castle up high.

Traditional
Action is limited at this time. Assistance in the near future will be welcomed. Unable to make a move at this time. Lack of direction makes actions difficult. Not able to see all that's needed to move forward. Limited resources to improve a situation.

Slight Shift
Refusing to see what's in front of you. Not wanting to make a difficult choice. Procrastination keeps you bound in a bad situation.

Quirky
This reminds me of Harry Houdini: bound, blindfolded, and surrounded by dangerous swords. What association can you make between this famous escape artist and your question?

Random Word Associations
How do you see this card as representing learning?
What word associations can you make with "Deny"?

The Swords - **Essence of Thought**

Nine
~ Attainment ~

The Swords - Essence of Thought

Nine
~ Consultation ~

Description
A man sits up in his bed grieving in the dark. Mounted behind him are nine swords. The quilt on the bed shows a design of red roses and mystical symbols. On the bed frame is engraved a picture of one man slaying another as if in a dual.

Traditional
A denial in thinking has been lifted away. An unpleasant truth is accepted and no longer ignored. Necessary coming to terms of the situation. Past perceptions are realized to be untrue.
 Blinders are taken away and reality sets in hard.

Slight Shift
The way to your happiness is a difficult path but necessary to travel. Facing this challenge will bolster your spirit. A time to make amends. Other viewpoints can be accepted. Not in a good position to see things clearly.

Quirky
The swords on the wall remind me of black lights that bother the mans eyes. What association can you make with black lights to your question?

Random word associations
How do you see this card as Attainment?
What word associations can you make with "Acceptance"?

The Swords - **Essence of Thought**

Ten
~ Completion ~

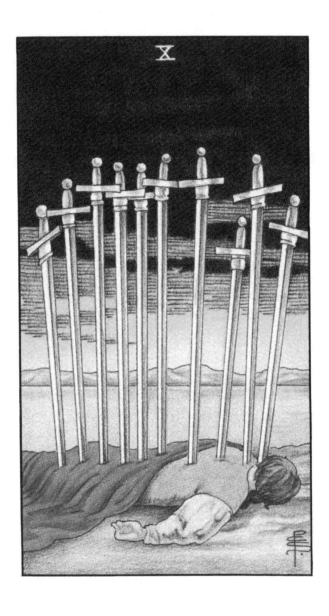

The Swords - Essence of Thought

Ten
~ Closure ~

Description
A man lays facedown with ten swords stuck in his body. The skies are dark, but there is light in the horizon showing the blue mountains and a peaceful lake.

Traditional
The end of a bad situation. A necessary loss lifts away burdens. Complete and finished resolve. Conflict can bring despair. A time to end negative aspects that are causing disruption.

Slight Shift
Caution on the issues is needed. Tread lightly with people's feelings. Touchy situations can get out of hand easily. Accept completion of the issue, and move on to a brighter environment.

Quirky
This reminds me of pincushions. They come in all different types of designs and colors. What association can you make between pincushions and other sewing equipment to your question?

Random Word Associations
How do you see this card as representing a completion?
What word associations can you make with "Cleanse"?

The Swords - **Essence of Thought**

Page
~ New Paths ~

PAGE of SWORDS.

The Swords - Essence of Thought

Page
~ Investigation ~

Description
A page stands fast, holding his ground against the wind. Ready for conflict, he holds a sword in both hands. The background shows clouds and trees blowing against him on a cloudy day.

Traditional
New direction. A chance for a better position on the issue. A new stance on an old issue. New thinking and new attitude. Seeing facts that are feasible to attain. Putting plans in place with positive intent.

Slight Shift
A different approach than previously used. New strategy. Time to change your stance on an issue. Another direction will work better.

Quirky
I'm seeing a left-handed baseball player standing at the plate waiting for the pitch. What association can you make between the game of baseball and your question

Random Word Associations
How do you see this card as representing a new path?
What word associations can you make with "Compass"?

The Swords - Essence of Thought

Knight
~ Action ~

The Swords - Essence of Thought

Knight
~ Execution ~

Description
A knight on a white steed charges forward with sword raised high. He is facing into the wind, and a storm seems to be on its way.

Traditional
Time is right to take action on a plan. Things will move forward if thought-out well. Resolve an issue now before it gets out of hand. Taking things into your own hands.

Slight Shift
The wind is about to change. Easy advancement on goals is made clear. You have your assets in place and are ready to proceed. Action now will be your best choice. Call others to your assistance.

Quirky
I'm seeing the Pony Express here, riding hard and fast to the next station with the mail. What association can you make between the Pony Express and your question?

Random Word Associations
How do you see this card as representing an action?
What word associations can you make with "Speed"?

The Swords - **Essence of Thought**

Queen
~ Patience / Understanding ~

The Swords - Essence of Thought

Queen
~ Perseverance ~

Description
On her throne, a queen sits in profile to us. In her right hand, she holds a sword upright as she holds her left hand out in a welcoming gesture. Clouds and wind seem to be blowing around her as she sits in the open air.

Traditional
Challenges are understood completely. Assistance is done with a logical approach. Ability to figure out a hard issue. Professional action based on solid thinking.

Slight Shift
Professional help is welcomed. Your ideas on a situation would be held with high regard. Offering your consultation and understanding will make others grateful.

Quirky
The clouds in this picture are down low instead of up high. I see her throne running by steam engine like old trains did. What association can you make between the steam engine and your question?

Random Word Associations
How do you see this card as representing understanding?
What word associations can you make with "Throne"?

The Swords - Essence of Thought

King
~ Knowledge ~

KING of SWORDS.

The Swords - Essence of Thought

King
~ Power ~

Description
A king holding a sword upright in his right hand sits erect on his throne. In the background are clouds and birds. The trees seem to be blowing in the wind.

Traditional
Advice and direction is acquired from the facts. Good grasp of a situation of concern. A position of authority. Experience is yours to share with those around you seeking advice. A wise choice is made.

Slight Shift
Attaining knowledge on the subject before acting would be beneficial. Consider all aspects and possibilities before you proceed. Think carefully before you act.

Quirky
The sword in his hand reminds me of the safety bar that goes across your lap on a roller-coaster ride. It will be pushed down horizontally across his lap before the ride starts. What association can you make between roller coasters or carnival rides and your question?

Random Word Associations
How do you see this card as representing knowledge?
What word associations can you make with "Grasp"?

The Cups

The suit of Cups' personality is one of deep feeling. People who are Cups have a knack for picking up what is not said. Cups feel people's energy easiest. Cups don't concern themselves as much with the facts as they do with the possibilities. Cups communicate to others with feeling. Cups sense their environment from the heart. Because of this, the Cups can become hopeless romantics. They are trusting and sincere partners. Cups are sensitive to the feelings of others. Cups are very imaginative. Like all the suits, Cups can make wonderful mates.

The suit of Cups is the water sign. The suit of Cups can also represent the emotional aspects of things felt in your life. The Cups are the power of empathic and intuitive energy.

In Relationships: Cups value relationships of deep bonding from the heart. A soul mate.

The Cups - Essence of Emotion

Cups value:
Being enthusiastic
Trusting intuition
Yearning for romance
Seeking identity
Prizing recognition

Swords value:
Being calm
Trusting reason
Yearning for achievement
Seeking knowledge
Prizing deference

Wands value:
Being excited
Trusting impulse
Yearning for impact
Seeking stimulation
Prizing generosity

Pentacles value:
Being concerned
Trusting authority
Yearn for belonging
Seeking security
Prizing gratitude

Oz Personification: *The Tin Man*

The Cups - Essence of Emotion

Ace
~ New Concept ~

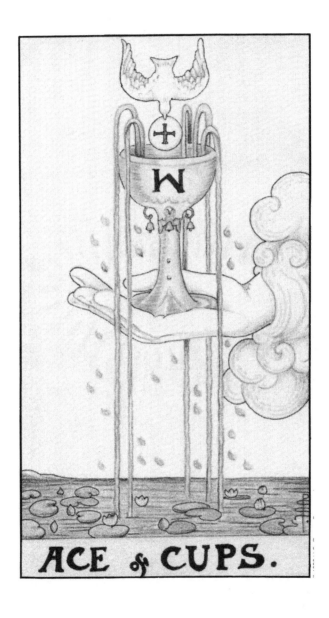

The Cups - Essence of Emotion

Ace
~ Empathy ~

Description
A hand holding a golden chalice comes out of a cloud. A dove swoops down from overhead with a wafer marked with a cross in its beak. Five streams of water flow from the chalice into a lake below.

Traditional
A new concept from the heart. New relationship. A strong feeling from an outside influence. A love of self creates a love from another. A new love is in the making. A friendship overflows into a loving commitment.

Slight Shift
A relationship has shifted to the better. Time has created a new sense of happiness with another. A loyal partner.

Quirky
Call the plumber! I'm seeing this cup leaking. What association can you make between plumbers or other tradesmen and your question?

Random Word Associations
How do you see this card as representing a new beginning?
What word associations can you make with "Lover"?

The Cups - Essence of Emotion

Two
~ Choice ~

The Cups - Essence of Emotion

Two
~ Commitment ~

Description
A young couple stand facing each other as if in loving ceremony. They each hold a cup as the man holds the woman's hand in his. The caduceus of Hermes raises between them with a winged lion's head. In the background is a peaceful setting with a house on a hill.

Traditional
Deeply felt choices are made.. Sincere offers of love could be mutual. The decision for a new level of friendship or relationship. An agreed-upon commitment. A common ground is established.

Slight Shift
A choice is made to move forward with feelings toward another. Deep bonds. Personal communication. Deep interaction between two people. A new relationship.

Quirky
I'm seeing two people hypnotized by the flying lion head above them. What association can you make between hypnotism and your question?

Random Word Associations
How do you see this card as representing a decision?
What word associations can you make with "Agreement"?

The Cups - Essence of Emotion

Three
~ Creativity ~

The Cups - Essence of Emotion

Three
~ Nurturing ~

Description
Three maidens dance in celebration. They all raise their cups to honor a happy occasion. The bounty of a harvest lays at their feet.

Traditional
Celebrating a heartfelt situation. A new level in feelings. Mutual agreement is understood. Honoring of a relationship. Creating a new mutual heartfelt arrangement. Learning and experiencing another's true essence.

Slight Shift
Anniversaries. A new measure of commitment. Festivities. Happiness of a situation. Recognized success.

Quirky
The woman on the far right is holding a bunch of grapes. That reminds me of grape jelly and peanut-butter-and-jelly sandwiches for lunch in the kitchen. What association can you make between things found in the kitchen and your question?

Random Word Associations
How do you see this card as representing progression?
What word associations can you make with "Party"?

The Cups - Essence of Emotion

Four
~ Stability ~

The Cups - Essence of Emotion

Four
~ Conformity ~

Description
A lone figure sits under a tree gazing at three cups before him. A fourth cup floating in midair is held by a hand coming out of a cloud.

Traditional
A stable environment. Calm and reflective. All going as planned. No noticeable changes are expected. Predictable outcome. No sudden surprises for now.

Slight Shift
A tendency to become lax. Opportunity could be missed out. Not seeing everything that's happening in your surroundings. Good intentions are offered but not accepted.

Quirky
I'm seeing Isaac Newton sitting under the apple tree. Soon an apple will fall on his head. What association can you make between gravity and your question?

Random Word Associations
How do you see this card as representing inactivity?
What word associations can you make with "Steady"?

The Cups - Essence of Emotion

Five
~ Change ~

The Cups - Essence of Emotion

Five
~ Resignation ~

Description
A man wearing a long black cape sadly looks down at three cups spilled before him. Two more cups remain upright behind him. A river flows before him, and a home is in the distance.

Traditional
Change resulting in loss. A situation could be in jeopardy. A situation threatened with failure. Reversal of an unpleasant set of circumstances may be difficult. A stable situation is in jeopardy.

Slight Shift
Necessary purging of a bad predicament. Painful release for the good. Not all is lost. Salvage what can be kept. A time to heal and move forward.

Quirky
I'm seeing Batman without his mask. What association can you make between the Caped Crusader to your question?

Random Word Associations
How do you see this card as representing change?
What word associations can you make with "Purge"?

The Cups - Essence of Emotion

Six
~ Overcoming Obstacles ~

The Cups - Essence of Emotion

Six
~ Generosity ~

Description
Two children exchange kind affection. The little boy gives the little girl a flower that's placed in a cup. She is looking at him with kindness. Another cup rests behind the boy, and four more are in the foreground.

Traditional
Differences can be resolved with a new start. Seeing the other person's point of view. Starting over again. A new attitude is in the making for the better. Success in overcoming challenges of the heart. Understanding both sides of the situation.

Slight Shift
Things begin to look better. Time has helped heal a negative issue. Intentions are genuine. A new start of an already established relationship.

Quirky
I'm seeing St. Valentine's Day in a grammar school. What association can you make between St. Valentines Day and your question?

Random Word Associations
How do you see this card as representing accomplishment?
What word associations can you make with "Child"?

The Cups - Essence of Emotion

Seven
~ Confidence / Ability ~

The Cups - Essence of Emotion

Seven
~ Progress ~

Description
A man comes out of the shadows and sees many cups before him. Each cup contains curious objects, and all are clouded in smoke.

Traditional
New awareness on your issue brings about many options. A need to look at all possibilities before taking action. Confidence in the issue brings many speculations. Rewards because of sincere efforts.

Slight Shift
Hard choices overwhelm you. Things are just coming into perspective on a matter from the heart. Take time to regroup before you decide. Coming out of the dark. Seeing the possibilities.

Quirky
I'm seeing the man in the dark as a pantomime. What association can you make between pantomimes or other street performers to your question?

Random Word Associations
How do you see this card as representing ability?
What word associations can you make with "Clouds"?

The Cups - Essence of Emotion

Eight
~ Awareness / Learning ~

The Cups - Essence of Emotion

Eight
~ Modification ~

Description
A man walks away from eight cups through a rocky, watery landscape. Mountains are in the distance, and the moon is in the night sky.

Traditional
More is needed to complete a heartfelt goal. Time spent searching will get positive results. You are missing some pieces to the puzzle, but you will find the answers if you look. Setting your feelings in place before acting would be wise.

Slight Shift
Taking a different position will show you a new approach and solution. Don't get stuck thinking one way only. Solutions are close by if looked for.

Quirky
The cups in the foreground remind me of a jigsaw puzzle with one piece still missing. What association can you make between puzzles and your question?

Random Word Associations
How do you see this card as representing learning?
What word associations can you make with "Rocks"?

The Cups - Essence of Emotion

Nine
~ Attainment ~

The Cups - Essence of Emotion

Nine
~ Prosperity ~

Description
A content man relaxes in comfort on a bench. Behind him are nine cups resting on a curved table with a blue tablecloth.

Traditional
A goal is completed. Success in your pursuits. Accomplishment. Satisfaction. A time to enjoy what has been accomplished. Abundance and contentment.

Slight Shift
A time to breath easy. No pressure. Life is easy-going. Life is good. Lighthearted environment. Happiness for a job well done.

Quirky
I'm seeing a security guard sitting in front of a blue-curtained archway entrance. What association can you make between security guards and your question?

Random Word Associations
How do you see this card as representing attainment?
What word associations can you make with "Coffee"?

The Cups - Essence of Emotion

Ten
~ Completion ~

The Cups - Essence of Emotion

Ten
~ Devotion ~

Description
A family is enjoying their setting and acknowledging a rainbow of ten cups in the sky. Their happy home sits on a hill in the background.

Traditional
Appreciating your accomplishments. Joy and happiness. A history with another is established. Reputation and trust has survived the test of time. A completion from the heart.

Slight Shift
A focus on the long-term goals. Planning security for retirement. A loving environment. Enjoying another stage of a lasting relationship.

Quirky
I'm seeing Fourth-of-July fireworks instead of cups in the sky. The family is enjoying the fireworks display. What association can you make between the Fourth of July and your question?

Random Word Associations
How do you see this card as representing completion?
What word associations can you make with "Firecracker"?

The Cups - Essence of Emotion

Page
~ New Paths ~

PAGE of CUPS.

The Cups - Essence of Emotion

Page
~ Variables ~

Description
A page stands near a shore. He gazes into a cup containing a fish, which he holds in his right hand. Waves appear in the background.

Traditional
An offer coming from the heart. A new approach will open new doors. An intuitive concept can bring options. A keen imagination will help you reach your goals.

Slight Shift
The ability to truly feel concepts clearly. Be careful of illusions or false perceptions. An unusual set of circumstances make unusual choices necessary.

Quirky
I'm seeing a magic trick: pulling a fish out of a cup instead of a rabbit out of a hat. What association can you make between magicians (and their acts) to your question?

Random Word Associations
How do you see this card as representing new paths?
What word associations can you make with "Fish"?

The Cups - Essence of Emotion

Knight
~ Action ~

The Cups - Essence of Emotion

Knight
~ Engagement ~

Description
A knight with a winged helmet holds a cup in his right hand and he rides forward on his steed A gentle river runs alongside high mountains in the distance.

Traditional
True and heartfelt action is taken to create peace and happiness. An act of kindness. A show of concern and care. Direct and clear focus moves forward on an inspirational goal. Heartfelt initiative moves things forward.

Slight Shift
Good possibilities if taken slowly. Promising and peaceful solutions are available. Planning a positive environment from the heart will be recognized.

Quirky
The wings on his ankles and helmet make me think of FedEx. His cup is a package being delivered. What association can you make between overnight shipping and your question?

Random Word Associations
How do you see this card as representing action?
What word associations can you make with "Kind"?

The Cups - Essence of Emotion

Queen
~ Patience / Understanding ~

The Cups - Essence of Emotion

Queen
~ Graciousness ~

Description
A queen wearing a golden crown and admiring an elaborate cup sits on her throne. In front of her is a lake. A cliff is in the distance.

Traditional
A strong sense of compassion. A good understanding from someone who cares deeply. Waiting for the right time to move forward. Clear focus stemming from a wise source.

Slight Shift
Too much focus on only a part of the issue. A need to see the bigger picture. Loving eyes cannot see.

Quirky
I'm seeing an antique collector with a newly acquired piece. What association can you make between antiques and your question?

Random Word Associations
How do you see this card as representing understanding?
What word associations can you make with "Prizes"?

The Cups - Essence of Emotion

King
~ Knowledge ~

KING of CUPS.

The Cups - Essence of Emotion

King
~ Tact ~

Description
A king sits on a throne floating in a sea. He is holding a scepter in his left hand and a cup in his right. Around his neck he wears an amulet of a fish. A sailing ship is off in the distance.

Traditional
A good knowledge of a heartfelt situation. Care from a wise authority. A loving ally has answers to your questions and concerns. Sound decisions can be made. Decisions are made for the better of all.

Slight Shift
A need to know more about the facts. Seek outside opinions regarding the goal at hand. More insight will create a better end-result. A solution coming from deep feelings will manifest.

Quirky
I'm seeing the king sitting in a recliner with a beer in one hand, a TV remote in the other and ready to watch the Super Bowl. He's also not wearing any shoes. What association can you make between objects found around the TV and your question?

Random Word Associations
How do you see this card as representing knowledge?
What word associations can you make with "Water"?

4. Card Spreads

THE MAP OF YOUR QUESTION

A card spread is a map of your question. It is a map of factors that directly pertain to the question being asked. Card spreads are set up in a consistent pattern with numbered positions. A card spread allows you to look at a particular question in segments or factors that pertain to the issues in question. It allows you to look deeper into all the aspects intuitively. The fact that you are seeing your question in a visual way is important as well. It makes things clearer than outlining a list of concerns or possible solutions. A tarot card is then randomly placed into each position of the card spread and associated with the factor of that position. I will be giving three example readings for each of the card spreads shown in this chapter.

I have placed the Quick Reference List at the start of this chapter again for easy reference. All of the sample readings supplied in this chapter are fictitious and are just to show clear examples. The example readings themselves have been purposely kept to simple and basic issues. The purpose of the examples are to show procedures and not to offer counseling advice. My hope is to explain the procedures clearly with as little confusion as possible.

Quick Reference List: The 22 Major Arcana

Number	Card	Meaning
0	The Fool	New Beginnings
1	The Magician	Awareness / Consciousness
2	The High Priestess	The Subconscious / Hidden
3	The Empress	Creativity
4	The Emperor	The Builder
5	The Hierophant	Spiritual Guidance
6	The Lovers	Duality / Choice
7	The Chariot	Success / Ability
8	Strength	Self-Direction / Self-Control
9	The Hermit	Inner Searching
10	The Wheel	Evolvement
11	Justice	Truth
12	The Hanged Man	Sacrifice
13	Death	Transition
14	Temperance	Inspiration
15	The Devil	False Hopes / Fears
16	The Tower	Rude Awakenings
17	The Star	Hope and Guidance
18	The Moon	Mysterious Paths
19	The Sun	Nurturing / Enlightenment
20	Judgement	Resurrection / New Awareness
21	The World	Perfect Balance / Harmony

Note: Some Tarot decks have the Strength and the Justice cards numerical value transposed. Justice still keeps its meaning of "Truth", and Strength still keeps its meaning of Self-Direction / Self-Control.

Quick Reference List: The 56 Minor Arcana

Number   **Card Meaning**

Aces.................................. New Concept
Twos................................. Choice
Threes............................... Creativity
Fours................................ Stability
Fives................................. Change
Sixes................................. Overcoming Obstacles
Sevens.............................. Confidence / Ability
Eights............................... Awareness / Learning
Nines................................ Attainment
Tens.................................. Completion

Pages................................ New Paths
Knights............................. Action
Queens.............................. Patience / Understanding
Kings................................ Knowledge

Essence of the Four Suits:

Pentacles/*Diamonds*.................The Physical
Wands/*Clubs* ....The Spirit
Swords/ *Spades*.........................Thought
Cups/*Hearts*..............................Emotion

Note: I have used a common definition for all four cards of each
suit. The suit definition will show you how the card is defined specifically. Example: Aces are defined as "New Concept". Therefore,
the Ace of Swords would be a new concept in your thinking. The
Ace of Cups would refer to a new concept in your emotions. The
Five of Wands would represent a "Change" in your spirit. The Five
of Swords would call attention to a "Change" in thinking—and so
on.

Who's who?

Most books today call the person sitting across from you, getting the reading, the querent. You, of course, are called the reader. Older books still in circulation might call the person sitting across from you the "questioner." Some works will call the person "the seeker."
Over the years the term "seeker" has always fit best in my pocket.
In *Genius of the Tarot* the person you are reading is called the "seeker" or "client".

Procedures to a card reading.

There are many ways to handle a card reading. Everyone seems to have their own method that works best for them. Here is mine. Only I shuffle my cards, not the seeker. I then place the deck in front of the seeker and ask them to cut it into three packs. I then turn over the top card of each pack. Now I have three packs with the top card of each pack facing up. I then ask the seeker their question. After hearing their question, I decide which of the three top cards seems most appropriate to the question being asked. I use that pack for the card spread and the other two remaining packs are set aside and out of play. I place that top card in the first position of the spread and continue by placing cards from that pack in the remaining positions of the spread. I lay out the complete spread before I start reading. All cards are placed face-up in the spread. All cards face me.

The Four Suits

A client comes to you with the suit already decided. They come with an issue from the heart, *Cups*. An issue of reason, *Swords*. An issue of spirit, *Wands*. Or an issue of a material concern, *Pentacles*.

I mainly see the four suits of the Minor Arcana as representing the four basic personality types. This can help tell me much about a person sitting across from me in a reading. Sensing the make-up of a person can greatly increase your ability to help them achieve what they seek to accomplish.

Fluently reading Tarot.

The Three Card spread is also a good way to learn to read Tarot fluently. Fluent reading is reading the cards effortlessly as you are laying them out in a spread. It's continuous and moves smoothly. This is spontaneous and very intuitive. It also makes the reading flow nicely when applied. It is a good way to start the reading before looking into each card in depth. Just speak what you see as you are laying each card out. The more you get to know the cards, the smoother it will flow.

The Three-Card Spread

The best way to learn how to read cards is to practice the Three Card Spread. The Three-Card Spread helps you to see the cards working together. It's important to see how the cards can interact with each other. The Three-Card Spread shows this very well. It's very basic and easy to learn. It also can be very efficient. It's usually used for a quick answer. Three cards are placed face-up from left to right, facing you. Learning to read three cards in combination instead of separately can be very helpful in making your reading flow nicely. In order for the cards to speak, they have to interact with each other in some way to make a statement. Combining cards will make sentences that pertain to the question. This also helps you shift a cards meaning to fit with the other cards. Sometimes one card will have to adjust a little to fit in with the other two to have an overall meaning. Typically, the position factors for this spread are *past, present* and *future*. However, these factors can be changed to something more specific and meaningful to the question being looked into. An example might be "*strengths, weaknesses*, and *opportunity*." Remember that the factors are segments to your question. And the question is the most important part of the reading. The more specific the questions factors are, the more specific the answer can be.

Three-Card Spread –   **Example #1**

I want to show how three cards can make a statement by working with each other. In this example, the question will be asked about a relationship that is having troubles. The client is looking for ways to salvage the situation. We will use the Three-Card Spread standard factors of past, present, and future for this example.

Past   Present   Future

The cards drawn:
Page of Pentacles
Four of Cups
Temperance 14. – *Major Arcana*

The cards that were drawn are the Page of Pentacles, the Four of Cups, and Temperance. You might see their meaning slightly differently than I do. I might see this differently tomorrow. That's the point. No two people will see things exactly the same way. Any constructive advice seen is coming from your intuition but still can be grounded with rational thinking.

Three-Card Spread – **Example #1**

Interpretation: "This relationship initially showed a lot of promise, but as it progressed, it became drab and routine. Focus on putting inspiration back into this relationship. The Four of Cups shows inaction, which is what caused this drifting apart—no action taken in any positive way to strengthen the relationship. But fortunately, inaction also means no serious actions were taken in a negative way either—no infidelity or words that can't be taken back. Respect and trust are still felt, but with a loss of interest. No bridges were burned. They're just not used anymore. Act with inspiration, and you will receive inspiration back."

Meanings Defined
Page of Pentacles — *new paths*
Four of Cups — *stability*
Temperance 14 — *inspiration*

The Past: the Page of Pentacle—new paths shows "Initially things went well."

The Present: the Four of Cups—Stability shows inaction.

The Future: Temperance — Inspiration.

Wrapping it up: "Initially things went well enough, but over time things became drab, even boring. Putting some inspiration back into the relationship will renew interest. Striving for a common challenge that can be shared together can help make things right again."

Three-Card Spread – **Example #2**

In this example the client's question is about a job change.

I decided to change the factors of the question to something geared more to careers. So instead of factors past, present, and future, we will use strengths, weaknesses, and opportunities.

Strengths   Weaknesses   Opportunities

The cards drawn:
Ten of Cups
The Tower 16 – *Major Arcana*
Six of Swords.

The cards that were drawn are the Ten of Cups, The Tower, and the Six of Swords. Notice how the suit doesn't seem to make much difference to our question? The Cups in the first card would deal more with love than career. But the number ten has meaning. This is why I feel the suit is secondary in reading cards. The suit has already been decided in the question itself. Career change is the question. Pentacles, not Cups, might be a better suit for career change.

Three-Card Spread – **Example #2**

Interpretation: The Ten of Cups shows a completion in your knowledge and skills—an accomplished person who knows their profession very well. Your experience is your strength. The Tower shows that you were involved in a bad business decision. Prepare to be asked about this in future interviews. If you choose to make a move, your experience with challenging situations will be welcomed by a company you will be employed by. This is shown by the Six of Swords -Overcoming Obstacles.

Meanings Defined

Ten of Cups—*completion*
The Tower 16—*rude awakenings*
Six of Swords—*overcoming obstacles*

Strengths: the Ten of Cups—completion shows "your experience."

Weaknesses: The Tower—rude awakenings shows "Prepare to explain a bad decision from the past in a positive way."

Opportunities: the Six of Swords—overcoming obstacles shows "You will be hired because of your experience with challenging situations." (I intuitively added the Six of Swords as a time frame of six months as well.)

Wrapping it up: Think of your past as a strong point. You have faced hard challenges which has taught you much. Your seasoned experience seems to be key in acquiring the new position. Plan on this transition to take place within the next six months.

Three-Card Spread – **Example #3**

In this example the client's question is "I would like to open up a coffee house. Is this a wise idea?" Here again, past, present, and future seem to be moot points to this question. So I will replace those factors with timing, location, and strategy.

Timing   Location   Strategy

The cards drawn:
Two of Wands
Five of Swords
The Devil 15– *Major Arcana*

The cards that were drawn are the Two of Wands, the Five of Swords, and The Devil. Changing the factors isn't necessary, but it does help broaden the intuitive insight the cards can give you. It can also help give you a better focus to the question at hand.

Three-Card Spread – **Example #3**

Interpretation: The Two of Wands shows the timing looks good to make choices toward your pursuits of happiness. The Five of Swords shows to look for a location where change is happening—a town that is building up quickly. The Devil in strategy's position shows a place that people can avoid idleness and get things accomplished—wireless Internet, pads of paper with your logo, and a cup of pencils provided at each booth and table. Also, fast service near a train station would be beneficial. The Devil is also a reminder for you to check everything carefully before signing a lease. Be leery of offers that seem too good to be true. Illusion and procrastination are both forces seen by the Devil card.

Meanings Defined

Two of Wands—*choice*
Five of Swords—*change*
The Devil 15—*false values*

Timing: the Two of Wands—choice shows "You are ready."

Location: the Five of Swords—change shows "Look in towns that are building up quickly."

Strategy: The Devil—false values shows "Focus on your coffee house being a place where people can accomplish their business without pro-crastination,. Also be wary of commitment to a contract or lease before you find out all the facts."

Wrapping it up: This is a big choice. Focus on a location where big changes seem to be happening to open your doors of business. A place where people can get things accomplished as they have a cup of coffee.

The Four-Winds Card Spread

A card spread is the randomness of 78 cards placed into various sections of your question. What is unique about the Four Winds spread is instead of just turning over a fifth and final card for the last position, it tells you what card should be placed there. This is accomplished by adding up the values of all four cards in play to find a fifth and final card for added insight. The Four Winds card spread only uses the 22 Major Arcana. This card spread allows you to see a question from all aspects of your consciousness. Your *thinking, feeling, spirit,* and *physical* world. The four positions are North, South, East and West, symbolizing the four corners of your world.

The 22 Majors are shuffled, and one is randomly placed in each of the four positions face up. The order of placement is N, S, E, and W. The North position allows you to look at your question from a rational, logical perspective. The South position allows you to look at your question with your feelings and emotions. The East allows you to look at your question from your soul—your inspirations. The West allows you to look at your question from a physical/material standpoint.

Each Major Arcana is numbered. An example is The Magician, which is #1, The Hermit is #9, The Moon is #18, and so on. After you have read the meanings of the card in their assigned position, you add up the cards' numbers. If the number is higher than twenty-one, you would add the new numbers together to equal another number until you have a number that is twenty-one or lower.

Example: The four cards drawn are The Empress, #3 ; The Devil, #15; The Hermit, #9; and Temperance, #14. That totals 41. We need a number of 21 or lower, so we now take 41 and add the two numbers again: $41 = 4+1 = 5$.

 The Hierophant is #5 and we place that card in the center for additional advice, a possible solution, or confirmation in response to the question.

~Position Factor~
Logic/Thought

~Position Factor~
Physical/Material

~Position Factor~
Spirit/Inspire

~Position Factor~
Feelings/Emotion

The Four-Winds Card Spread

In the North position we have the Empress, number #3 of the Major Arcana: we associate the factor position of *logic/thought* with the question.

In the South position we have the Devil, number #15 of the Major Arcana: we associate the factor position of *feeling/emotion* with the question.

In the East position we have the Hermit, number #9 of the Major Arcana. We associate the factor position of *spirit/inspiration* with the question.

In the West position we have Temperance, number #14 of the Major Arcana. We associate the factor position of *physical/material* with the question.

In the Center position we have The Hierophant, number #5 of the Major Arcana. We associate the factor position of something key to the question for additional advice or insight.

Seeing the cards in this spread for their symbolism can also show you much without even using the factor positions.
Seeing the factor positions as one aspect in this spread and then just reading the cards for what they can tell you for more insight seems to work best for me with this spread. Also keep in mind you can always change the factor positions to your liking.

The Four-Winds ~   **Example #1**

We will now use these same cards for the first example reading.

Question: Should I open a restaurant?

North position is my *reason/logic* toward the question.
Card: The Empress, #3, shows creativity and growth in a concept.
I'm in a good financial position to move on this quest. The market is
right to buy. The time seems right to create the situation.

South position is my *feelings/emotions* toward the question.
Card: The Devil, #15, shows false fears and procrastination. My feelings are "I'm afraid of investing and ultimately failing."

East position is my *spirit/inspiration* toward the question.
Card: The Hermit, #9, shows inner searching—a need to look deep
within myself for the answer. Is it what I really want in life? Would
having a restaurant truly fulfill my dreams?

West position is the *physical/material* aspects of the question.
Card: Temperance, #14, shows inspiration. Success would be uplifting
and inspiring. I would feel good about myself. The timing looks good
to create the restaurant. Inspiration and pride would be in place if the
restaurant became a reality.

Now we add up the cards:
3+ 15 = 18 + 9 = 27 + 14 = 41; 4 + 1 = 5

The Hierophant, #5, is placed in the center and read for additional
random insight.

~*Position Factor*~
Logic/Thought

~*Position Factor*~
Spirit/Inspire

~*Position Factor*~
Physical/Material

~*Position Factor*~
Feelings/Emotion

The Four-Winds ~   **Example #1**

Center position indicates "Something Key to the question"

Card: *The Hierophant, #5*, means spiritual guidance. Here we will slightly shift the card's meaning from spiritual guidance to just plain guidance. Professional assistance would be helpful from someone who knows the restaurant business before you act on this issue.

Wrapping it up: Looks like you're in a good position right now to act on your goal. Timing looks good too. Looking for additional guidance on this matter will help your fear of failure. The more you know, the more confident you will feel. Ask yourself if a restaurant is really the business you want to have. Your entrepreneurship might lead you in another direction. Looking into things deeper might help you find the right business for you. Getting some outside advice might shed new light on this endeavor.

THE EMPRESS.

TEMPERANCE.

THE HIEROPHANT.

THE HERMIT.

THE DEVIL.

The Four-Winds ~   **Example #2**

Question: The client is contemplating a new relationship. She wants to know if it looks promising.

North position is my *reason/logic* toward the question.
Card: Justice, #11, shows truth. You're thinking clearly and seeing all the facts as positive. Things seem honest and sincere.

South position is my *feelings/emotions* toward the question.
Card: The Magician, #1, shows consciousness. Your feelings are awake, and you are in a good position for a successful, heartfelt relationship, with no confusion from the heart by either of you.

East position is my *spirit/inspirations* toward the question.
Card: The Tower, #16, shows rude awakenings. A history of heartache puts a cramp on your spirit for love. As the relationship moves forward, that will tone down and be replaced with trust from the logic of the Justice card.

West position is the *physical/material* aspects of the question.
Card: The Moon, #18, shows mysterious paths. The relationship will be good as it creates itself with things not yet discovered. The physical aspects of this mate will click well with you as they become known. Things look good. Don't let past failures stop you from finding happiness. Having trust in yourself and your new partner is key.

Now we add up the cards:
11+ 1 = 12 + 16 = 28 + 18 = 46; 4 + 6 = 10

The Wheel of Fortune, #10, is placed in the center and read for additional random insight.

~Position Factor~
Logic/Thought

~Position Factor~
Physical/Material

~Position Factor~
Spirit/Inspire

~Position Factor~
Feelings/Emotion

The Four-Winds ~   **Example #2**

Center position indicates "Something Key to the question"

Card: The Wheel of Fortune, #10, shows evolvement. If you proceed, the Wheel shows movement in positive ways. The two of you
will benefit from each other's strong points. This possible relationship
looks like a positive move.

Wrapping it up: It seems that the time is right for both of you to
become involved. Truth and confidence are strong in this arrangement.
Plan on things to continue moving in a positive direction. Both of you
have seen conflict with past partners but trust will overcome any hesi-
tations to move forward with this one. Plans on taking this relationship
to another level will move forward by October. This is shown by the
number ten in the Wheel of Fortune.

The Four-Winds ~   **Example #3**

Question: The client is offered a different job. She wants to know if the move would be a wise choice.

North position is my *reason/logic* toward the question.
Card: The Fool, #0, shows new paths. Follow your heart on this. Don't overthink the situation. Keep a carefree attitude. No job is ever guaranteed.

South position is my *feelings/emotions* toward the question.
Card: The Hanged Man, #12, shows self-sacrifice. Giving up the friendships of co-workers will open doors to new opportunities and friends.

East position is my *spirit/inspiration* toward the question.
Card: The World, #21, shows perfect harmony. It looks like the change would be very rewarding for your spirit. It has the possibilities to even influence your life outside of work.

West position is the *physical/material* aspects of the question.
Card: The High Priestess, #2, shows subconsciousness. A feeling of happiness will be in the air at the new workplace. Peace of mind will stay with you even after you leave the building. You were offered this new position because, deep down, you were looking for a change. If further interviews go well, the move seems like a winner.

Now we add up the cards
0 + 12 = 12 + 21 = 33 + 2 = 35; 3 + 5 = 8

The Strength card, #8, is placed in the center and read for additional random insight.

~Position Factor~
Logic/Thought

~Position Factor~
Physical/Material

~Position Factor~
Spirit/Inspire

~Position Factor~
Feelings/Emotion

The Four-Winds ~   **Example #3**

Center position indicates "Something Key to the question"

Card: Strength, #8, shows inner strength. It takes courage to make a job change. You leave a secure position and take on another not knowing what's ahead. But it's a necessary move if you feel you may be happier at the new place. Not going will only make you all the more frustrated with your current position. If you feel something's missing in your job, then it's time to move on.

Wrapping it up: This opportunity came to you because you were innately looking for a change. The World card seems to scream yes. Happiness is yours with this move. The Enchantress in the Strength card shows you will do well on your new journey.

NOTE: When adding the numbers together, you may end up with a final number being a card already in play. An example would be a final number in the previous example adding up to 11, The Hanged Man. But the Hanged Man is already in use in the south position. If this happens, you would add the cards again only without adding the Hanged Man into the mix. In other words, the above would be adding The Fool, The High Priestess, and The World cards only: 23; 2 + 3 = 5. The Hierophant #5 would be your fifth card going in the center

The Celtic-Cross Card Spread

The Celtic Cross consists of two parts: the cross, numbers one through six, and what is called the pillar, numbers seven through ten. There are many ways to do a Celtic Cross. If you look into it, you will see the ten position factors vary from one source to another in dramatic ways. But just like card definitions, all spreads are viewed differently by different users. Don't let that bother you. Which one works the best for you? The one that appeals to you the most. It's as simple as that. What's important is that they all work fine. It just comes down to a personal preference. I will be showing one way I use a Celtic Cross in the following three examples. Afterwards, I will show two other popular Celtic-Cross spreads with different position factors.

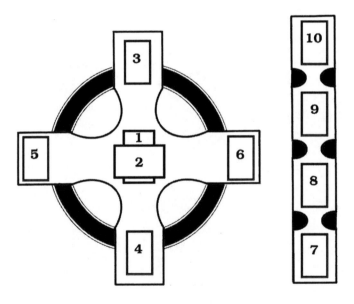

The Unseen Map of the Question

I would like to mention the importance of a card spread before we
begin. A card spread is a map of the question. It exist on your table
without you seeing it. You don't see it until answers (cards) are placed
into it, but it is there. You always have the option of changing the position factors of the map to your liking. We did this in the Three Card
Spread examples. I would suggest drawing the spread out on paper to
create a visual image for you to look at. Getting to know your spread
well will help you see meaning in the cards easier as they are placed
into each position. I also suggest sticking with one spread. I think it is
best to know one spread exceptionally well than a number of spreads
in a mediocre way. The Celtic Cross is a good sound spread capable
of answering any question. It is the only spread I use on a professional
basis. The position factors of any spread is what will make the spread
effective. As you may see from the following examples, I'm also
partial to the Three Card Spread. The Three Card Spread, by itself, is
always a good spread for a glance at a question. And the position factors are easy to change for each question.

What, Why, How and When

I feel the Celtic Cross speaks to me best as four important aspects to
look into: *what, why, how,* and *when*.
First, it allows the reader to check how the client is seeing their own
question. If the client is not seeing the whole picture or is disillusioned
about the situation, it can be questioned and called to his or her attention. Second, for what purpose or end does the client want this goal?
Third, it gives us the ability to question what the client can do to
achieve this goal. We can question the client's strategy for achieving
the goal. And fourth, it allows us to look at the timing of the issue. Is it
time to act now, or would taking action at a later date be in the client's
best interest?
The ten positions of the Celtic Cross will be looked at as the four aspects to your question. What, Why, How and When. The first three of
the four aspects use three cards each. Like a Three Card Spread previously explained, leaving one card left to read by itself as the fourth and
final aspect of Timing (When).

The Celtic-Cross Card Spread continued

This is another reason why explaining the Three-Card Spread was important. However, the cards are not grouped in order, another words they are not read as #1,#2 and #3 as the first group, #4,#5 and #6 as the second group, #7,#8 and #9 as the third grouping, leaving #10 by itself for the timing of the question. Over time the selected groupings I use just happened on it's own as time went by. No matter how you do a Celtic Cross spread, certain positions just seem compatible with certain other positions. They just naturally fall in line with each other. An example is the first grouping of #1,#2 and #7. Most sources explaining the Celtic Cross will imply in some way that positions #1 and #2 represent the actual question itself while position #7 represents the client in relation to their question. Therefore, when doing the Celtic Cross, that grouping naturally shows the client's association to his or her own question, making them compatible as a group.

The Celtic Cross pattern itself is not that important. You could get the same results by simply laying three rows of three cards left to right. It just wouldn't be a Celtic Cross design anymore.

The groupings are
Group One: #1,#2 and #7
Group Two: #3, #4 and #9
Group Three: #5,#6 and #10
By Itself: #8

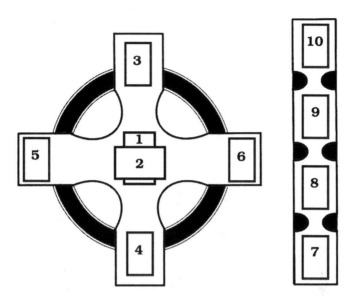

Cards #1 and #2: these two positions combined are a view of
the question.

Card #3: what the client is going through
Card #4: what the client is trying to achieve
Card #5: an asset the client should utilize
Card #6: an opportunity coming in the near future
Card #7: the client's viewpoint of his or her own question
Card #8: the timing factor—time to act, or time to wait?
Card #9: what's the client ultimately trying to achieve?
Card #10: possible positive and negative aspects to watch for.

The Celtic-Cross Card Spread continued

We look at the Celtic Cross as cards #1 and #2 being separate from the rest of the spread. They are read together to make a statement about the question being asked. We look at these as a confirmation of the real question being looked into. Those two positions make us take a close look at the question itself. The remaining eight other positions are aspects or factors of the question.

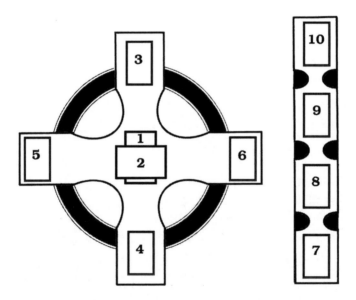

A more in-depth look at these positions would be as follows.

Positions #1 and #2 – Working together, these two cards represent the question itself.

Position #3, - Represents what the client is going through, meaning what the client is going through to achieve a goal.

Position #4 – Represents the goal itself

Position #5 - Represents an asset or advantage the client may have in helping to achieve a successful outcome.

Position #6 - Represents an opportunity, in the future, to utilize the advantage or asset found from the #5-position..

Position #7 - Represents how the client is seeing their own question. This gives the reader a chance to check that the client isn't being unrealistic about the goal or question—that he or she isn't seeing a bad situation as a good one or visa-versa.

Position #8 - Represents the timing of the issue in question. Is it a good time to act? Or should you let things be for now?

Position #9 – Represents what the client is ultimately trying to achieve in the larger scheme of things. The client might want to achieve the goal, of the #4 position because he or she thinks it will give them the big picture of position #9 . Why do they want this goal?

Example: *Position #4* might be, "I want a pay raise."
Position #9 might be, "I really just want to be happy with my job."

Position #10 concludes what's been covered in the reading: a wrap-up. It's a reminder to have the client walk away with a plan and a direction. It shows what can be achieved or what can be avoided if chosen to.

The first example will be a client is thinking about a job change.

Celtic-Cross Card Spread – Example #1

Finding the facts

Don't hesitate to ask your client questions. Get as many facts possible. The more you know to begin with, the more you can focus on a solution.

Client: Mr. G.
Age: Forty-two
Occupation: Graphic designer
Married: Eighteen years. Two children, sixteen and fourteen years of age respectively

The Question: I have a secure, well-paying position at a major advertising agency downtown. But the hours are long, the stress is high, and the commute is time-consuming. This leaves me no quality time to enjoy my family or pursuits of interest. All I do is work. An associate is opening up a small advertising agency right in my home community and has offered me a position. The hours would be regular, nine to five, and the commute is only twenty minutes. I have twenty years seniority in my current job, with good salary. The pay would be less if I take the new job offer. And I'm concerned about the new company making it in this competitive advertising market today. I would be taking a risk with job security. The new company will be in place in three months. Any ideas or suggestions?

Cards that were drawn
1) Nine of Wands
2) King of Cups
3) Five of Wands
4) Knight of Swords
5) The Lovers
6) Two of Cups
7) The Devil
8) King of Wands
9) Nine of Pentacles
10) Ace of Cups

Celtic Cross ~   **Example #1**

First Grouping – #1,#2 and #7:

~ What? ~

Attainment, Knowledge and Fears of moving forward –
are shown in the cards drawn.

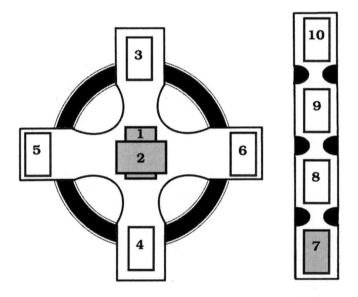

1. Nine of Wands—definition: *Attainment* (the question)
2. King of Cups—definition: *Knowledge* (the question)
3. Five of Wands
4. Knight of Swords
5. The Lovers
6. Two of Cups
7. The Devil—definition: *False fears* (client's viewpoint)
8. King of Wands
9. Nine of Pentacles
10. Ace of Cups

Celtic Cross ~   **Example #1**

First Grouping – #1,#2 and #7:

~ What? ~

Attainment, Knowledge and Fears of moving forward –
are shown in the cards drawn.

Positions #1 & #2: The Question

Position #7: Client's perception of their own question

A close look at the true question.
What the client sees or needs to see.

Interpretation:
So far we realize the client is not as stuck as he thinks he is.
He has attained through the Nine of Wands, the Knowledge of the
King of Cups. An opportunity because of his experience and knowl-
edge. But he sees the situation with a sense of shaky ground through
the Devil card. He has the knowledge and could attain what he seeks.
The Devil card shows a false fear of loss and self-limitations.

Celtic Cross ~   **Example #1**

Second Grouping – #3, #4, and #9:

~ Why? ~

*Changes, Action and Attainment
are shown in the cards drawn.*

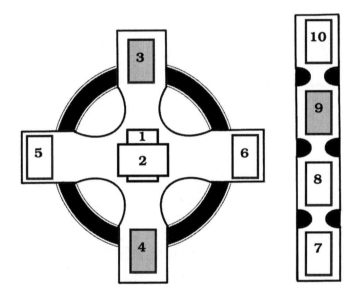

1. Nine of Wands
2. King of Cups
3. Five of Wands—definition: ***Change*** (currently going through)
4. Knight of Swords—definition: ***Action*** (trying to achieve)
5. The Lovers
6. Two of Cups
7. The Devil
8. King of Wands
9. Nine of Pentacles—definition: ***Attainment*** (ultimate goal)
10. Ace of Cups

Celtic Cross ~   **Example #1**

Second Grouping – #3, #4, and #9:

~ Why? ~

Changes, Action and Attainment
are shown in the cards drawn.

Position #3: What the client is going through

Position #4: What the client is trying to achieve

Position #9: The clients ultimate goal

What the client is doing. What the client is trying to accomplish.
Why do you want this? What is the ultimate goal?

Interpretation:
It seems as if the client would like to make a change with the Five of
Wands. His actions are a tell tale sign with the Knight of Swords. This
might be effecting his work as well. He seems to realize attaining his
ultimate work place with the Nine of Pentacles is out of reach in his
current position.

Celtic Cross ~   **Example #1**

Third Grouping — #5, #6, and #10:

~ How? ~

Duality shows opportunity and a choice made to take the new position is being shown in the cards drawn.

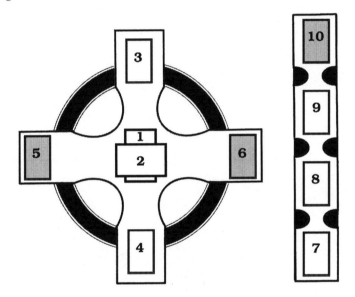

1. Nine of Wands
2. King of Cups
3. Five of Wands
4. Knight of Swords
5. The Lovers — definition: ***Duality*** (an asset)
6. Two of Cups — definition: ***Choice*** (an opportunity)
7. The Devil
8. King of Wands
9. Nine of Pentacles
10. Ace of Cups — definition: ***New concept*** (possible result)

Celtic Cross ~   **Example #1**

Third Grouping— #5, #6, and #10:

~ How? ~

Duality shows opportunity and a choice made to take the new position is being shown in the cards drawn.

Position #5: An asset the client has

Position #6: An opportunity

Position #10: Possibilities

What advantages does the client have?
What opportunities should the client look for in the near future?
How can the client use these resources for a successful outcome?

Interpretation:
We can see with the Lovers card that he is faced with the duality of staying in his secure but unhappy state or moving on. He is in a good position to make a change. We can also see the Lovers card literally as his wife's support in his decision. The Two of Cups shows the opportunity to make a change is confirmed to come as offered. The choice will remain as planned. The Ace of Cups shows the new place of employment will probably be accepted.

Celtic Cross ~   **Example #1**

Position #8 — Timing:

~ When? ~

Capability is shown in the card drawn.

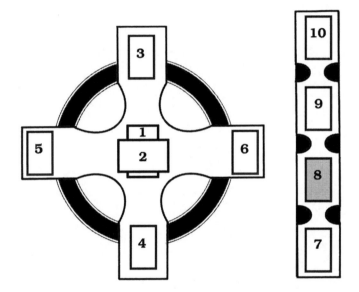

1. Nine of Wands
2. King of Cups
3. Five of Wands
4. Knight of Swords
5. The Lovers
6. Two of Cups
7. The Devil
8. King of Wands — definition: ***Knowledge*** (the timing of issue)
9. Nine of Pentacles
10. Ace of Cups

Celtic Cross ~ **Example #1**

Position #8—Timing:

~ When? ~

Capability is shown in the card drawn.

Position #8: Time to act? — Or time to wait?

When is the best time to act?

Interpretation:
Here we have the King of Wands (knowledge). This could be taken in a few ways. One would be a need to gather more knowledge before you act. Another would be you have all the knowledge now, so go ahead and make your choice today. But seeing we started this reading with the King of Cups in the #2 position, and we now are looking at another king, the King of Wands in the #8 position, it makes me think that it would be a good time for this king to change his image.

Wrapping it up: The timing seems good to make the change in jobs. I feel you have a lot to offer to this new company, and you will have the freedom to enjoy other aspects of your life you are now missing. Don't let life pass you by. Give your present employer an ample two month notice to find a replacement. I see you leaving on good terms. Then take a month to spend with your family before you start your new journey!

Celtic-Cross Card Spread – Example #2

Keep it simple:
As the reader, all cards face me.

The client: Ms. M.
Age: Thirty-one
Occupation: Bank teller (associate's degree in business)
Single: Dating Mr. C.

Question: I have been seeing Mr. C. for three years, but the relationship seems to be drifting apart. Am I losing him? I feel he doesn't seem interested anymore.

The cards that were drawn:
1. Knight of Cups
2. Seven of Pentacles
3. Three of Cups
4. The Moon
5. Death
6. Queen of Pentacles
7. Page of Cups
8. The Hanged Man
9. The Tower
10. Justice

Celtic Cross ~   **Example #2**

First Grouping – #1,#2 and #7:

~ What? ~

*Action , Accomplishment and New Direction –
is shown in the cards drawn.*

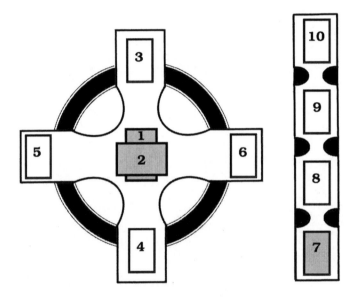

1. Knight of Cups—definition: *Action* (the question)
2. Seven of Pentacles—definition: *Success/Ability* (the question)
3. Three of Cups
4. The Moon
5. Death
6. Queen of Pentacles
7. Page of Cups—definition: *New paths* (client's viewpoint)
8. The Hanged Man
9. The Tower
10. Justice

Celtic Cross ~   **Example #2**

First Grouping – #1,#2 and #7:

~ What? ~

Action , Accomplishment and New Direction –
is shown in the cards drawn.

Positions #1 & #2: The Question

Position #7: Client's perception of their own question

A close look at the true question.
What the client sees or needs to see.

Interpretation:
The Knight of Cups shows new actions are in play but the
Seven of Pentacles shows me the relationship is still successful.
The Page of Cups confirms your concerns of a new path manifesting.
A negative path threatening the relationship. The Knight joined with
the Page shows a strong bond with the Seven of Pentacles. The rela-
tionship has good potential. So far the change seems to be coming
from a source other than the relationship.

Celtic Cross ~   **Example #2**

Second Grouping – #3, #4, and #9:

~ Why? ~

A newly created awareness of unknown circumstances needs to be addressed – is shown in the cards drawn.

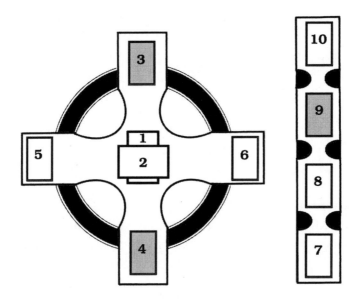

1. Knight of Cups
2. Seven of Pentacles
3. Three of Cups — definition: *Creativity* (currently going through)
4. The Moon — definition: *Mysterious paths* (trying to achieve)
5. Death
6. Queen of Pentacles
7. Page of Cups
8. The Hanged Man
9. The Tower — definition: *Rude awakening* (ultimate goal)
10. Justice

Celtic Cross ~   **Example #2**

Second Grouping – #3, #4, and #9:

~ Why? ~

A newly created awareness of unknown circumstances needs to be addressed – is shown in the cards drawn.

Position #3: What the client is going through

Position #4: What the client is trying to achieve

Position #9: The clients ultimate goal

What the client is doing. What the client is trying to accomplish. Why do you want this? What is the ultimate goal?

Interpretation:
The Three of Cups is generating a lot of creative ideas. Too many! It could be jumping to conclusions at this point. The Moon card shows the path is not clear, but that card is usually a sign of an unknown but ultimately good direction non-the-less.. The Tower shows conflict and struggle, but not necessarily pertaining to you. Things need to be ironed out to be right again.

Celtic Cross ~   **Example #2**

Third Grouping— #5, #6, and #10:

~ How? ~

*Major change in your understanding will show the truth –
is shown in the cards drawn.*

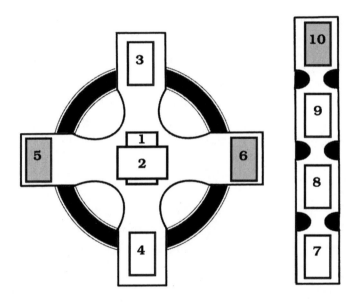

1. Knight of Cups
2. Seven of Pentacles
3. Three of Cups
4. The Moon
5. Death—definition: ***Transformation*** (an asset)
6. Queen of Pentacles—definition: ***Patience*** (an opportunity)
7. Page of Cups
8. The Hanged Man
9. The Tower
10. Justice—definition: ***Truth*** (possible result)

Celtic Cross ~   **Example #2**

Third Grouping— #5, #6, and #10:

~ How? ~

*Major change in your understanding will show the truth –
is shown in the cards drawn.*

Position #5: An asset the client has

Position #6: An opportunity

Position #10: Possibilities

*What advantages does the client have?
What opportunities should the client look for in the near future?
How can the client use these resources for a successful outcome?*

Interpretation:
The Death card shows me the client fears a major change in the relationship. She can get through this trying time. She will have a better understanding of the problem soon from the Queen of Pentacles. Patience for now is key. The Justice card shows truth will prevail and all will be explained in the end. Believe in the relationship.

Celtic Cross ~   **Example #2**

Position #8 — Timing:

~ When? ~

Inaction is shown in the card drawn.

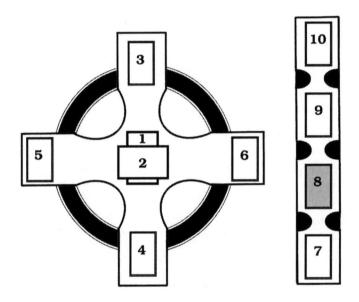

1. Knight of Cups
2. Seven of Pentacles
3. Three of Cups
4. The Moon
5. Death
6. Queen of Pentacles
7. Page of Cups
8. The Hanged Man — definition: *Sacrifice* (the timing of issue)
9. The Tower
10. Justice

Celtic Cross ~   **Example #2**

Position #8 — Timing:

~ When? ~

Inaction is shown in the card drawn.

Position #8: Time to act? — Or time to wait?

When is the best time to act?

Interpretation:
Sometimes timing can mean everything. Here we have the Hanged Man. He seems perfectly content with his situation. This is a time to put away fear and doubt. Like the Hanged Man, see things from a different point of view. You have the ability to change your thinking if you try. Inaction is best for now.

Wrapping it up: Mr. C. does have a troubled mind right now, but it's no reflection on you. Something else is troubling him. This is probably work-related. Could be stress seen in the Tower card. Focus on the friendship of the relationship for now. Intuitively, I see the Moon card showing me things should be back on track by the next full moon. After the dust has settled let him know he should share issues on his mind with you more. After all – you are his partner and these are things you need to know.

Celtic-Cross Card Spread – Example #3

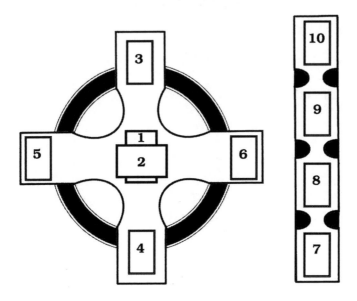

Clients and your cards.

Everyone has their own way of going about doing a reading.
I start by shuffling the cards and then I ask the client to cut
the deck into three packs. I then turn over the top card, face up on
each pack. I then ask the client their question. Based on their answer,
I choose the pack who's top card seems the most appropriate to the
question to use for the card spread.

The client: Ms. K.
Age: Fifty-five
Occupation: Owns a hair salon
Relationship: A one-year relationship

Question: A year ago I met a man who was separated and going through a divorce. After one month's time, we were in love. At least he said he was. The divorce still hasn't happened, and I'm starting to feel he's having second thoughts.

The cards that were drawn:
1. Judgement
2. Six of Cups
3. Queen of Cups
4. Five of Wands
5. The High Priestess
6. The Star
7. Eight of Swords
8. Ace of Wands
9. Ten of Swords
10. Four of Swords

Celtic Cross ~　　　**Example #3**

First Grouping – #1,#2 and #7:

~ What? ~

New awareness and learning to take on challenges –
is shown in the cards drawn.

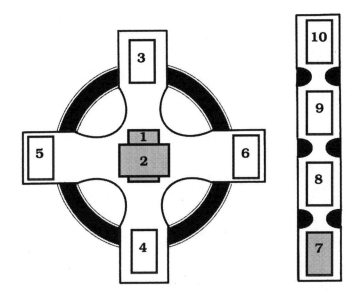

1. Judgement—definition: ***Evolvement*** (the question)
2. Six of Cups—definition: ***Overcoming obstacles*** (the question)
3. Queen of Cups
4. Five of Wands
5. The High Priestess
6. The Star
7. Eight of Swords—definition: ***Awareness*** (client's viewpoint)
8. Ace of Wands
9. Ten of Swords
10. Four of Swords

Celtic Cross ~   **Example #3**

First Grouping – #1,#2 and #7:

~ What? ~

New awareness and learning to take on challenges –
is shown in the cards drawn.

Positions #1 & #2: The Question

Position #7: Client's perception of their own question

> *A close look at the true question.*
> *What the client sees or needs to see.*

Interpretation:
It seems like the Eight of Swords is learning to see this situation in
a different light than it was initially. The Judgement card shows new
awareness is taking place within his marriage.
And the Six of Cups shows overcoming challenges from the heart
within the marriage which is putting challenge on your relationship.

Celtic Cross ~   **Example #3**

Second Grouping – #3, #4, and #9:

~ Why? ~

*A change and completion will come with a new understanding –
is what's shown in the cards drawn.*

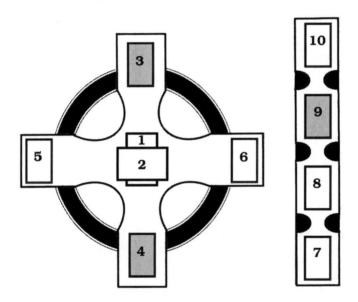

1. Judgement
2. Six of Cups
3. Queen of Cups - definition: *Patience* (currently going through)
4. Five of Wands - definition: *Change* (trying to achieve)
5. The High Priestess
6. The Star
7. Eight of Swords
8. Ace of Wands
9. Ten of Swords - definition: *Completion* (ultimate goal)
10. Four of Swords

Celtic Cross ~   **Example #3**

Second Grouping – #3, #4, and #9:

~ Why? ~

*A change and completion will come with a new understanding –
is what's shown in the cards drawn.*

Position #3: What the client is going through

Position #4: What the client is trying to achieve

Position #9: The clients ultimate goal

*What the client is doing. What the client is trying to accomplish.
Why do you want this? What is the ultimate goal?*

Interpretation:
The Queen of Cups shows a time of testing patience as time goes on.
The Five of Wands shows anticipating changes in the relationship.
The Ten of Swords shows a completion because of difficulty in moving forward.

Celtic Cross ~   **Example #3**

Third Grouping — #5, #6, and #10:

~ **How?** ~

*Finding answers within self will bring about a healthier
direction. A locked, stable, relationship without you –
is shown in the cards drawn.*

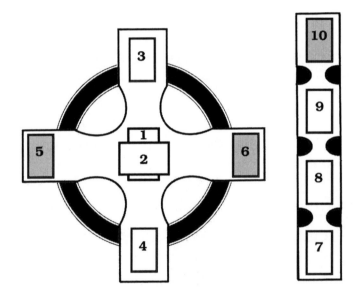

1. Judgement
2. Six of Cups
3. Queen of Cups
4. Five of Wands
5. The High Priestess — definition: ***Subconscious*** (an asset)
6. The Star — definition: ***Hope*** (an opportunity)
7. Eight of Swords
8. Ace of Wands
9. Ten of Swords
10. Four of Swords — definition: ***Stability*** (possible result)

Celtic Cross ~   **Example #3**

Third Grouping— #5, #6, and #10:

~ How? ~

Finding answers within self will bring about a healthier direction. A locked, stable, relationship without you – is shown in the cards drawn.

Position #5: An asset the client has

Position #6: An opportunity

Position #10: Possibilities

What advantages does the client have?
What opportunities should the client look for in the near future?
How can the client use these resources for a successful outcome?

Interpretation:
The High Priestess tells innately you are sensing an end.
The Star shows a time of new direction is to come soon.
The Four of Swords shows his marriage will remain stable.
Deep down the seeker knows that the situation is changing, and hope for a solution in her favor is fading. It's hard for her to face, but it seems his marriage will remain and become stable again.

Celtic Cross ~   **Example #3**

Position #8 — Timing:

~ When? ~

*A new beginning. A fresh start –
is shown in the card drawn.*

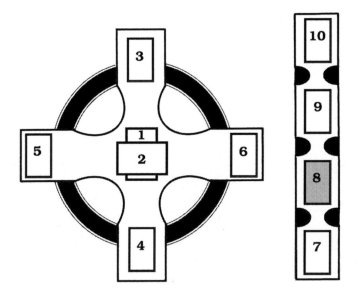

1. Judgement
2. Six of Cups
3. Queen of Cups
4. Five of Wands
5. The High Priestess
6. The Star
7. Eight of Swords
8. Ace of Wands—definition: ***New concept*** (the timing of issue)
9. Ten of Swords
10. Four of Swords

Celtic Cross ~   **Example #3**

Position #8—Timing:

~ When? ~

A new beginning. A fresh start –
is shown in the card drawn.

Position #8: Time to act? — Or time to wait?

When is the best time to act?

Interpretation:
The Ace of Wands shows a time to start new. A completion, an end of one cycle and the beginning of another. Things are falling into place for a fresh start.

Wrapping it up: This has no reflection on you. You didn't lose him; you never really had him to begin with. When he told you he loved you, he meant it. But the words came from a confused person who was on an emotional roller coaster. This is a time to end the relationship with him. However, you have much to offer in a healthy relationship. Once you heal from this one, I see love coming into your life once again. This time it will be a relationship that will come without any confusion attached to it. Let this one go, but do it in a friendly and for-giving fashion. Understanding his confusion with a sense of care will help ease your pain and will quicken your healing.

Celtic-Cross Using a Different Set of Position Factors

The position factors we have been using for the Celtic Cross can be changed. Here is another set of meanings for each position that would be helpful for a reading.

Celtic Cross Using a Different Set of Position Factors

Positions #1: The question itself

Positions #2: A look at the question from another viewpoint

Positions #3: What could be improved about "self" to succeed

Positions #4: How you can start changing things in your favor

Positions #5: What attributes do you have available—are you using all of them now?

Positions #6: What changes need to take place for you to succeed

Positions #7: Why do you want this goal in your life?

Positions #8: When and how is the best time to act

Positions #9: What challenges do you need to understand on this question?

Positions #10: A focus of the completed goal and how to get there: a wrap-up

I created these position factors for a client of mine specifically. But I feel the position factors could be beneficial in most readings. They are read individually instead of three-card runs as previously. They still cover what, why, how, and when, only with a different approach than we used in our sample readings.. The positions are pretty self explanatory and the cards are looked into individually and deeply instead of in combination with other cards. Although three-card runs help create flow in your reading, this method can find very deep answers just as well. Over time you may come across many different approaches to the Celtic Cross. What works best for you will bring the best results in the end.

The Celtic Cross with Traditional Position Factors

Lastly I am including a Celtic Cross with classical, traditional position factors.

The Celtic Cross with Traditional Position Factors

Positions #1: this covers the client—an influence at this time

Positions #2: this crosses the client—an obstacle

Positions #3: this is above the client—the best possible outcome

Positions #4: this is below the client—the real base of the question

Positions #5: this is behind the client—the past

Positions #6: this is before the client—immediate future

Positions #7: this is the client at this moment in time—his or her perception of the question

Positions #8: this is the client's surroundings—family influences

Positions #9: these are hopes and fears—what the client anticipates

Positions #10: the completion—a finalization

This is a classic Celtic Cross which seems to have an approach based on fate and destiny rather than options or free will. Although I personally do not believe in fate or destiny I still think it's a great card spread. Try asking a question using all three of these samples, and see what works best for you. It really just comes down to a personal preference.

A good way to see this spread:
If you like the idea of fate and destiny, think of fate and destiny as the cards you were dealt in life. How you play those cards is still your free will.

5. Mind-Set of a Card Reader

Questions and Answers

As a reader, time is what we look at: the future of a question. Questions come from the present. Answers are found in the future. If the answer is already here, it no longer becomes an answer. It becomes a known fact. Questions and answers come from two different points in time. A reader gives answers to questions and thus predicts the future. A simple example would be if I were to ask you what day it was, you might advise me by saying I need to find a calendar. I will find my answer there. Or intuitively you may "pick up" that I have a calendar in my kitchen on the refrigerator door and tell me that I will find my answer there. Once a question is answered, it doesn't exist anymore.

But what if the answer found was not the perfect answer, and a better one does exist? The genius mind thinks that way and will look for a different, better answer where most people will accept the original answer as acceptable and never give it further thought.

Procedures to a card reading

As mentioned in the previous chapter only I shuffle my cards, not the seeker. I then place the deck in front of the seeker and ask them to cut it into three packs. I then turn over the top card of each pack. Now I have three packs with the top card of each pack facing up. I then ask the seeker their question. After hearing their question, I decide which of the three top cards seems most appropriate to the question being asked. I use that pack for the card spread and the other two remaining packs are set aside and out of play. I place that top card in the first position of the spread and continue by placing cards from that pack in the remaining positions of the spread. I lay out the complete spread before I start reading. All cards are placed face up in the spread. All cards face me.

Various Types of Readings

As a reader, you will notice patterns: patterns in people as well as patterns in the issues people bring to your table. Patterns are used to predict future events in many ways. Weather patterns help predict weather. Stock-market patterns help predict future economic conditions. Marketing patterns help predict sales. If the FBI is looking for a criminal, they will use criminal-behavior patterns to predict the criminal's whereabouts or next move. Card readers use patterns as well. One pattern to keep in mind is that most people coming for a reading have an issue that is out of their control. If it was in their control, they wouldn't be paying you for a reading. They would be taking care of the problem themselves. This is why love is such a big topic at the card reader's table. *"Does he love me?"* is a common patterned question. *Will I sell my house soon? Is it a good move to take this new job? Will we have a baby?* These are all questions where the client has little or no control over the issue. Paying attention to outcomes is helpful in finding patterns to these kinds of common questions. Finding out some facts helps your looking into patterns too. You might be asked, *"Will we have a baby?"* You may ask the client, *"How long have you been married?" "Are you taking fertility pills?" "Is the relationship passionate?"* Facts like that are what patterns are based on, and over time you will have a stored insight as to what results certain patterns bring.

Serious Clients

For the most part, I read in four different types of environments. I do phone readings, carnivals / fairs, house parties, and I also give personal counsel. Personal counsel clients usually have a serious issue to discuss. Most will see you more than once during an issue that is going on in their lives. This might be weekly sessions for a few months to monthly sessions for a full year. Once the client and I have established a scheduled meeting time, weekly or monthly – each reading looks into what needs to be done for this session. Over time a trust is built as things progress. Having empathy for a client's concerns will help put you in her or his space. This will help you see the issue through the client's eyes and ultimately see your client through a difficult or anxious time.

You are counseling — intuitively counseling — and it's important to identify a client's concerns. If you read professionally, your clients will be people with real concerns, and they will be very happy to tell you all they can about their challenge. Many goals need to be taken in stages. Like layers of an onion. And each layer brings you closer to an end result. I find it best to give the client clear, distinctive advice with long and short term objectives for the session. This way my counsel is made clear and will be proven to be correct or incorrect over a specific time period. And that's that.

I find it best to start out the reading looking at the issue in terms of sound logic and reason. I feel this helps give the question a good foundation on which you can build intuitive insight. You work on the client's facts to find intuitive answers and options. Your reading will show your accuracy as the issue progresses in the client's days to come.

Ultimately what we are trying to do is find a solution to a concerning situation the client wants resolved. You, the reader, have the opportunity to help make a difference in the client's life. Readings are basically 90 percent common sense with a very important 10 percent intuition thrown in the mix. And that 10 percent intuition can go a long way in giving a client an edge in a situation. Intuition is like concentrated knowledge.

House Parties

House parties are fun. For the most part, you will meet a lot of wonderful people all having a good time. The host will usually invite you to eat and join in the fun. These kind of situations are usually filled with people just looking for entertainment. In order for everyone their to get a reading with you in a reasonable time frame, the sessions are quick and easygoing. I call them popcorn readings. This is where you will come across seekers who give you nothing specific to go on. Plan on the readings being more for fun and entertainment. For the most part, there are no serious issues to read into in these type of settings. In some ways, this actually can make your readings harder to do. Trust your intuition and have fun. You will surprise yourself as time goes on with how intuitive you can be.

Carnivals and Fairs

Here you will get a mix of both serious and party-type readings. The nights bring music and festivity and if you enjoy *"people watching"* this is a great setting. In Chicago, the days are hot and the nights are cool, especially around the lake! You will come across a wide range of personalities in these settings. Usually these are annual events, and if you are there every year you will have a lot of repeat customers telling you if you were accurate with last year's predictions. The more accurate you are, the more business you will have the following year. I enjoy doing all readings, but these types have a great energy about them. Besides, I like carny food, the colored lights at night, the sight of a Ferris wheel, and the camaraderie with the other readers.

Phone Readings

Phone readings are convenient for you and for the client.

You can end up giving a client readings on the phone for years at a time and never meet the person. I have phone clients I haven't seen face-to-face in over ten years who call me with various issues as they arise. When something comes up and they need a reading, they call. It's that simple.

6. Card Reading and Mind Maps

Definition of Mind-Set

A mind-set is a set of assumptions, methods, or notations held by one or more people that is so established that it creates a powerful incentive within these people or groups to continue to adopt or accept prior behaviors. - Wikipedia

Since the eighteenth century, our view of the tarot and how it is used is a good example of a mind-set. The tarot and its applications for card reading is thought of as something mysterious, mystical, magical, and, to some, even scary. But today we can see this classic craft as an ingenius creative thinking process called mind-mapping. When viewed in this new light, it all comes together as something that can be explained — and more importantly, better understood. And better understood means more efficiently used. When you understand something, you utilize it with freer expression. It allows you to leave the *safe zone* and work outside the system.

Mind-mapping gives you a visual understanding of your question. It is done by creating ideas in the form of pictures or graphics for a clearer look of a question.

Leonardo da Vinci, along with many other great thinkers throughout history, is well known for his use of this system. But it wasn't until the 1950s that mind-mapping actually became a psychological study. Since then we have a better understanding of its creative and intuitive value when we look at a question or predict a future result. Instead of a linear approach, mind-mapping allows you to look at your question visually. It breaks a question apart into sections, creating a diagrammatic map. It is a more visual, intuitive, and imaginative right-brained thinking process. Genius minds tend to think this way naturally. Others simply have to learn this process to apply it to their questions. Figures like Edison, da Vinci, Einstein, Galileo, Darwin, and Ford all saw how useful this procedure was, and they achieved their greatness with the help of employing mind-maps in their work. Mind-mapping allows you to have a conversation with your intuition. It's an idea-generator that can show you many possibilities and solutions to things you are looking into.

A mind-map breaks a question apart into sections I call position factors. Here we have a mind-map with eight position factors that are of concern to a question. But a mind-map can have more or fewer position factors, depending on the question's needs.

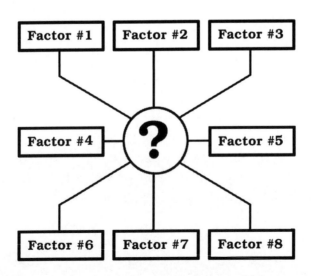

A mind-map's position factors are designed to be issues that will be helpful to your question. Position factors are things that directly pertain to the question being asked, and the factor's meanings would be decided by the maker of the mind-map. What is needed is a good question and then a number of factors that directly pertain to the question. The diagram of the map can be created in any way an individual chooses to make it, but usually the question is centered in the pattern, and the factors are positioned to surround the question in some fashion. You can then study the position factors, allowing you to focus on them in some manner to easily form new ideas or modifications for solutions to the question.

The cover of this book could be seen as an example of a mind map. In the center we have the basic concept, the title, and surrounding that we have factors about the book that can be easily seen and realized.

A card spread, like a mind-map, gives your question structure. It breaks a question apart into position factors as well and allows intuitive interrelationships between the sections in response to the question being asked. These interrelationships are seen in the cards that lay in each position factor of the card spread. The cards themselves interact with the various sections of the question to find formulas in regard to the question being asked or a concept being proposed. This structured but intuitive system allows readers to have a conversation with themselves using the right and left sides of the brain simultaneously to find unique, intuitive, and ultimately original and logical answers.

Card readings have been studied since the late eighteenth century, but, as I mentioned in the beginning of this chapter, mind-mapping has only recently been psychologically studied and recognized (since the 1950s). If you compare these two practices, you realize that they work in the same fashion. For centuries, we've had such strong, predetermined concepts of what a tarot reading is, we've never consider it as anything more. A tarot reading isn't mysterious. It's not an unexplained phenomena. A tarot reading works like a mind-map works.

The Celtic-cross card spread: A basic mind map with eight position factors.

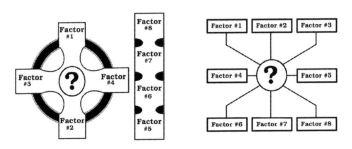

If we put cards spreads in the same category as mind-maps, we now can see them with an attitude of more freedom and personal expression. With this way of thinking, it frees up the card-reading immeasurably. This gives us a whole different perspective of unlimited possibilities available to us. Additionally, looking at a card spread in terms of mind-mapping brings a more solid foundation to the reading. It can mentally give the reading clear structure and open up many options to the way you approach questions and make future predictions. The strict attitude of customs like cutting the cards with only the left hand, reverse meanings, or laying the cards down in a specific, exact order seem to disappear. The process becomes free. Why? Because now we know what it is we're really doing and how it really works.

Facts:

Mind-maps attempt to look into the future of a situation.
Tarot readings attempt to look into the future of a situation.

Mind-mapping is used to solve problems or set up future objectives.
Tarot readings are used to solve problems or set up future objectives.

Mind-maps look at a question visually with patterned positions.
Tarot readings look at a question visually with patterned positions.

Mind-maps attempt to look into possible future options for the question.
Tarot readings attempt to look into possible future options for the question.

Mind-maps allow you to make a prediction on the future of a question.
Tarot readings allow you to make a prediction on the future of a question.

If it looks like a duck, walks like a duck, and sounds like a duck—it's a duck.

A card spread mimics the way the genius mind looks at a question.
A creative thinking process called mind mapping.

In a mind-map, random ideas are commonly associated into the various factor/sections of the question. This is done to give the question randomness. Randomness intuitively creates new ideas and associates the new idea to that particular factor of the question. Doing this allows us to come up with a new concept on that factor of the question. These random ideas can come from anywhere you choose. Randomly selected words from a dictionary would be an example. Another would be thinking of things found in the ocean. Then you would think of what attributes that random idea has that would help with this particular factor of the question. How would that attribute modify it or change it to something new and original? Make it better? Solve a problem? Allow me to see it differently?

A card spread is a map or diagram of a question, just like a mind-map. A question separated into sections. The sections are factors pertaining to the question.

The Tarot is a set of seventy eight random ideas meant to be placed into the various sections of the question. Each Tarot card has specific meaning that can be randomly associated to that particular segment of the question. This forces us to see the question differently in some fashion. Modify it, solve it, make it better than before.
It's a very creative application and it's very intuitive.

When you do a card reading, you are looking at a question the way a genius mind would look at the question. You are mapping it out and adding random ideas to each section of the map for new and original answers.
Today we would define that as a mind map.

Mind-maps are used to create or predict something that pertains to the future.

Tarot card readings are used to create or predict something that pertains to the future.

Both are accomplished by mapping the question out into sections and then adding random ideas to the sections for new and original ideas.

With a tarot reading, the random ideas that are placed onto the various sections of the card spread come from a deck of seventy-eight curious cards with dreamlike images we call the tarot.

If we define what is being done when doing a card reading, it would be the same definition of what is done when performing a mind-map.

If a process looks at a question in sections, visually, in a pattern, attempts to find constructive answers from this visual pattern, adds random ideas to the sections of the pattern to help modify preliminary answers for a new insight or answer, and does all this for the ultimate purpose of finding a possible future result, it is a mind map. It is also a tarot-card reading.

The Celtic-cross card spread: A basic mind map with eight position factors.

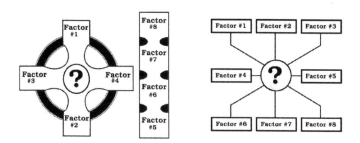

Positions one and two of the Celtic cross represent the question.

7. Tarot With A Twist

A Few Unusual Perceptions

A Picture Speaks a Thousand Words

Earlier in the book we talked about word association.

But the images of the Tarot can bring about other associations as well.

I want to show you how much we can find with just one card. The Tarot cards can be read in many ways: definitions, word associations, and the rich images themselves.

Question:
"Should I open a restaurant? And if so, what type and where?" We will use one tarot card to see what ideas it can tell us.

After shuffling, the card drawn was the Hermit, #9 of the Major Arcana.

Now, you might think, how can a hermit help with this question? Well, the trick is, we have to give him a chance.

The Hermit holds a lantern like a beacon—maybe that of a twenty-four-hour diner off a major expressway. The lantern reminds me of a big marquee that can be easily seen while driving on that expressway.

The Hermit is also wearing heavy garments. Is it cold where he is? How about if that twenty-four-hour diner is in the colder, northern part of the country—Minnesota, upper Wisconsin, or Michigan? The Great Lakes region?

The Hermit also holds a wooden staff. The wooden staff could be a hint as to location as well. Maybe the diner is near a national forest, lumber yard or somewhere else involving wood.

Answer #1:
The Hermit tells me to look for twenty-four-hour diners that are for sale with a big marquee sign right off a major expressway that has a paper mill close by, in the states of Minnesota, Wisconsin, or Michigan.

More coffee?

Another look:

The Hermit now will show us a different concept. The Hermit is secluded and private. He appears isolated and distant from others. How
about a restaurant that has very private settings, such as private rooms
instead of booths and tables? The Hermit's lantern makes me think of
candlelit ambiance: quiet, private rooms with candlelight or dim lighting. You order from a small computer screen on the wall that displays
the menu.

Once you select your order you click Send. A window comes up showing your room number and saying, "Your order has been taken. Thank
you." A light goes on outside the room above the door, showing the
waiters that you have made your order. The only time you see anyone
is when the food is served. No light on outside the door means you
don't need anything at this time. You can select the light to be on if
service is wanted. You can even pay your bill with a credit card from
the computer in the room.

Oh—of course the food is great too!

Answer:
A restaurant in a busy, northern city where people need some peace
and quiet, with private settings and a quiet atmosphere.
No waiter/waitress needed until food is served to you.
Check out and pay with a credit card from computer in room.

Fifteenth-century Dutch artist Hieronymus Bosch painting –
The Prodigal Son

The Tarot of Marseille: The Fool

The Fool card from the Tarot of Marseilles deck made
by Nicholas Conver of Marseilles,1761

The book cover

The cover of this book shows a painting by the renowned and mysterious fifteenth-century Dutch painter Hieronymus Bosch. He lived from 1450 to 1516—a time of the earliest tarot decks we know of today. The painting is called *The Prodigal Son*. At that time in history, the Holy Inquisition was in full strength. And heresy was a harsh sentence. Secret societies were necessary to share moral and spiritual views.

In Bosch's painting we see similarities to the Fool card in the Tarot of Marseille. The Tarot of Marseille is one of the most authentic tarot decks in circulation today. The deck is thought to have originated in northern Italy in the fifteenth century—the same time of Hieronymus Bosch. Bosch's Prodigal Son and the Fool from the Tarot of Marseille both show a traveler dragging along a staff and a snarling dog behind him. They both show tears in the traveler's pants as well. They also both carry a furry object attached to themselves. On the Tarot of Marseille Fool card this object is hanging from his tunic and seen against his right leg. This could be a tail of a cat. In the painting, it is a cat's skin hanging on the side of the traveler's basket. A cat's skin was considered a sign of bad luck in 15th century Europe.

And they both carry a spoon. In Bosch's painting the spoon is latched to his basket. And in the Marseille tarot card he carries his spoon over his shoulder with his possessions wrapped in a cloth tied to one end. No one ever seems to notice this curious detail on the tarot card. It was common for beggars to possess a large spoon in fifteenth century Europe. If they met someone cooking a pot of stew, they could approach them politely with spoon in hand and ask for a spoonful of stew.

What's interesting here is the basket on the back of the traveler in Bosch's painting. In the time of Bosch, when a young man reached a certain age, his mother would weave him a basket to wear on his back. He then would journey out into the world to experience more than just his village. In his travels he would acquire certain items to remember his journey by and tell his tale to his family and friends on his return. Today we use photo albums.

Once the young man returned home, his basketful of items would be hung on a nail on the wall next to his father's basket—and his grandfather's basket. The items from their travels were reminders of family history and stories could be shared for generations. On his way out the door, his mother would remind him to be careful and to stay out of danger, because if the young traveler gets robbed during his travels and loses his basket, coming home with a few useless possessions wrapped in a cloth, tied to a stick, he comes home with shame as a fool.

The tarot-card traveler carries no basket—just his spoon with a few belongings wrapped in a scarf tied at one end. Is that why this card is titled the Fool? I guess we'll never know for sure.

The Marseille deck also has the traveler wearing the garb of a court jester, with jingle bells on his collar and a floppy hat. Although fifteenth-century Europe still had court jesters, this was the time of the Renaissance. Maybe a court jester was considered by some to be an obsolete career? A fool's career.

Today most tarot decks depict this card in a much different light, as a carefree traveler moving forward, trusting that all is good. And the little dog is now his happy companion. He also carries no spoon in today's decks.

City Life and the fortune-teller in 18th Century Europe

The earliest records of card reading come from 18th century Europe.
Little information about the lifestyles of the common people at that
time is available today. Only the rich and famous seem to be remembered. By understanding the common citizens of that era we might get
a better picture of the typical fortune-teller of that period as well.

Well, you think you got it rough! Think again!

To understand the citizens of eighteenth-century Europe we need to
know what work was available at the time. London seems to have the
most on this subject. The jobs and lives of the working class was de-
plorable at best. At the upper end of income and comfort we have the
shopkeepers and artisans. These included upholsterers, coach painters,
joiners, watch-finishers to name a few. At the lower end of the "working class' were occupations now forgotten and barley recorded at all.
One example was the job called a "Pure-finder". The job was usually
done by old women. They walked the streets collecting dog waste
and sold it to tanneries for a few pence a bucket. The waste was used
to make a siccative in dressing fine bookbinding leather. There were
many occupational diseases. Sawyers went blind young, exposed to
so much sawdust it literally damaged their eyes. Metal founders died
paralyzed with lead poisoning. Glassblowers' lungs would collapsed
from silicosis. Hairdressers were susceptible to lung disease from
breathing the mineral powder needed to whiten wigs. Hatter's went
mad from using mercury nitrate to finish fine felt hats. Tailors, became
blind from eyestrain. The worst were the tailors of the military. The red
uniforms, for the English red coats with red thread was the hardest to
see in the poor lighting conditions of the times.

Prostitution and crime was in high numbers. The helpless begged
and thieves stole what they could. The gallows were full and one
could be hung for simply poaching a rabbit. Some of the slang terms
for those being hung for a crime were *"to dance upon nothing"*, *"the
morning drop"*, *"to take a leap in the dark"*, *"to loll your tongue
out at the company"* or, because of the strangling sounds made while
hanging, *"to cry cockles"*

The Industrial Revolution turned a blind eye to young labor. Orphaned children were forced to work in unhealthy, cruel conditions with physical, mental and emotional abuse for long hours without rest. Some to the point where the little ones would continue moving their hands in their sleep as if they were still working on the job.

The Industrial Revolution was the time of the card reader. If you were fortunate enough to own a deck of Tarot cards you could mystify the people with their magical images and your words of hope and destiny. I would imagine older women were the main card readers of the time. Maybe a "Pure-finder" by day and a card reader by night.
If I were a card reader back then I would want to protect myself and my cards with an air of mystical powers able to curse those who threaten to take what little money I had or worse yet, rob me of my cards.
I would also want to give the impression that only I could tap into the power of my cards assuring then that no one would try to take them from me. Yes, If I were an older woman card reader, I would want to appear as if I had magical powers that could read your mind and curse your very soul if I chose to.
In times like this what other protection would an old woman have.

Galileo and random ideas from a church.

Many great thinkers have associated random ideas to the questions they were looking into. What attributes does this random idea have that can be used in my question? Instead of looking in the obvious places for answers, when you choose something random, it forces new ideas to come up.

Time measurement was a major focus in many of Galileo's experiments.

Its importance was not so much for everyday living.

Without an accurate time piece, longitude could not be navigated at sea.

Galileo never stopped looking into this question of time keeping.

Then one day, in 1583 while sitting in the cathedral of Pisa he noticed the way the priest was swinging the incense filled thurible from its long chain during the mass. As it swung back and forth he realized this would be a good time keeping device. It is then that Galileo realized the potential of a pendulum for keeping time.

His concept would eventually be used in clocks. Although a pendulum clock must stand in a stable environment and could not be used on a sailing ship, it did become a standard time piece on land.

So as you look at the *Quirky* definitions in chapter three, remember Galileo and his quest of time keeping.

You can say that Galileo went into church that day in Pisa thinking "In what way can I associate things found in a church to my question of time keeping?" At first this may sound strange. But many new ideas do. Why? Because no one ever thought about them before.

Quirky? Yes. But the pendulum clock remained the most accurate time keeping device until the 20th century because of Galileo's discovery of the pendulum. He found that discovery by associating things found in a church to his question. That is intuitive. That is genius.

8. Three-Dimensional Card Spread

WARNING: This card spread is not for the faint of heart. See your physician before attempting this card spread. Do not attempt this spread while driving a car or operating heavy machinery.

This spread would be best used with a team of creative/ intuitive people. It's geared more to work on a project then a one-on-one type reading.

What's needed:

A large working area such as a conference table

One standard-size Rider Waite Tarot deck

One bridge-size Rider Waite Tarot deck (smaller version)

A blackboard or whiteboard.

You and your team will now list factors for the question to be looked into.

Example: The question is "Should I open a restaurant?"
Factor #1 might be "location."
Factor #2 might be "type of restaurant."
Factor #3 might be "liquor license?"
Factor #4 might be "hours of operation?"
 And so on.

In other words, things that would be important factors to your question. These would be your position factors: things that directly pertain to the question.

Using the standard-size deck, the spread initially starts out with a total of eight factor positions surrounding the centered question position (the same as a Celtic-Cross card spread). But instead of the pattern of the Celtic Cross, it is laid out to look like that on the following page. Using a blackboard near the table, list each position factor in a diagram, so everyone knows each factor position.

It's OK if you do not have eight factors; fewer can be used.

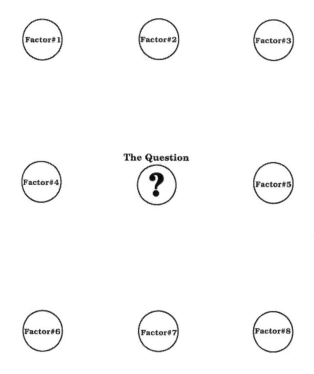

Randomly place two cards in the center of the table to represent the question. Next you would randomly place one card into each of your factor positions. Place all cards face up.

The team would discuss and barnstorm each card with the factor position it is placed into. You can associate the cards to the factor by its definition or by the image of the card itself or anything that it reminds you of—anything that pops into your head. After you have come up with some constructive ideas for each factor, you may now go even deeper if you choose.

This is done by using the smaller tarot deck, creating a second spread around each factor of the first spread. You could create just one new factor or up to eight new factors that pertain to the original factor.

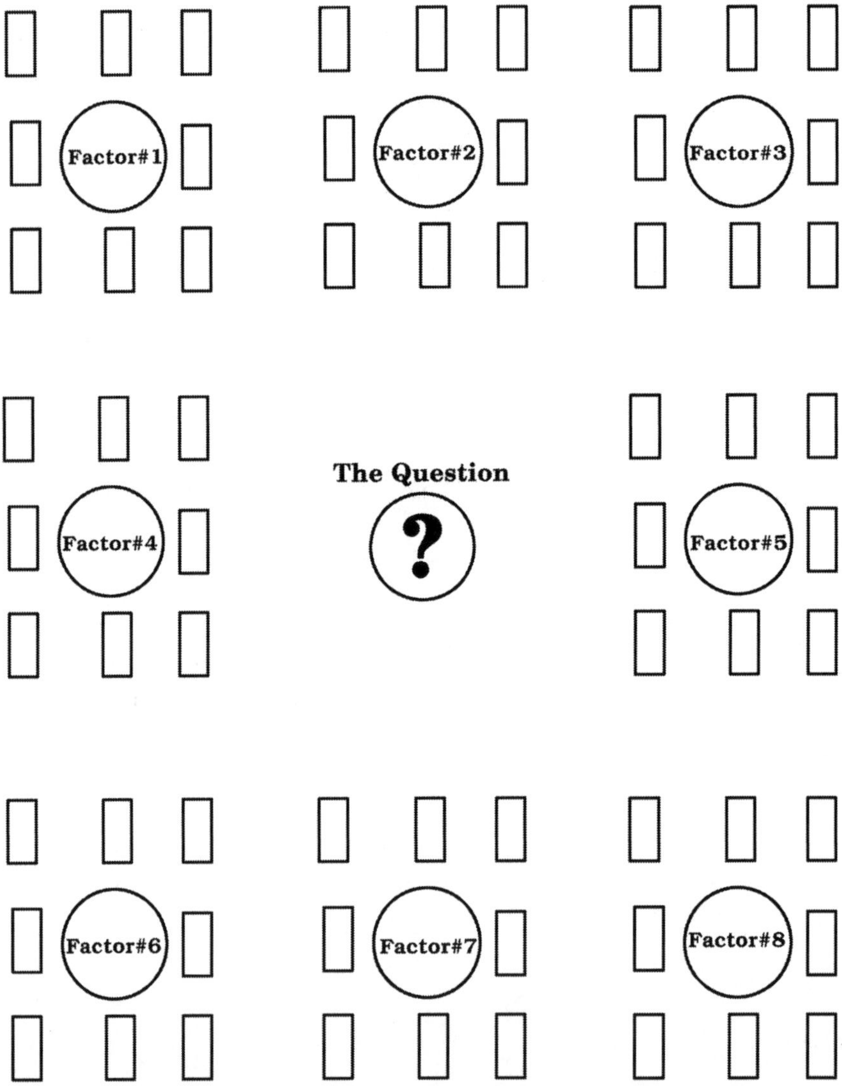

Factor#1

Factor#2

Factor#3

Factor#4

The Question

?

Factor#5

Factor#6

Factor#7

Factor#8

So factor number one would look like this if it had eight new factors: In the circle would be the card from the initial spread. The eight new positions surrounding it would use the smaller deck. The smaller deck's positions would use letters instead of numbers as shown in the picture below.

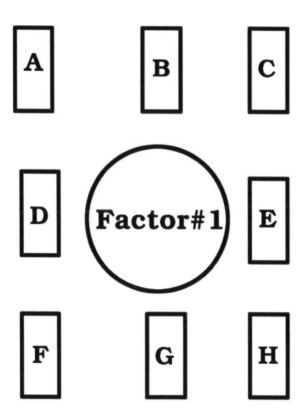

Go deeper? Let say you found something interesting to look into on position E. You can continue the process, going even deeper.

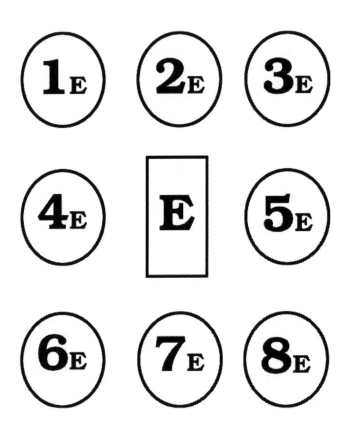

The more you look into the factors, the deeper you go, you will have a tendency to modify parts of them. You might substitute something in its place. You might reverse the way its applied. You might add something to it. The original factor might even become something different over time. This approach to a question would not be finished in an hour. It would be a longer process: a week, a month, or many months before decisions are finalized. But it allows you to look at a question in levels. You could use various objects or ideas combined with tarot cards. Maybe the diagram here would have a random word from a dictionary in section 6E instead of a tarot card. Or perhaps an object you would find in the desert listed in one or two of the factors instead of a tarot card. The reading may end up not using any tarot cards at all after awhile. Only using other random ideas in their place. Its' depth is infinite, and so is your imagination.

9. Conversations with the Cards

I could be tempted to get dramatic and call this "channeling", but it's not. It's just imagination gone a little wild. And it's just having fun. But it does help create imaginative relationships with the cards. The words in these conversations are not meant to be considered "gospel" as to what the card represents. They are meant to be seen as the card just letting their hair down. Sorta behind the scenes type of conversation. Having a conversation with one of the tarot cards can bring you new ways of seeing that card. It can give it personality, allowing you to relate to it on a personal basis. Visualize a visit from a card. What would it have to say to you – once it's off the job? I've put together five such visits to make up this last chapter. I hope you enjoy them and see the card in a different way afterward. To show how much the cards can change, I thought I would start out with a dark card: The Devil, #15

The Devil: Number 15
~ Misdirected Intentions ~

I hadn't been sleeping much, and now I'm just staring at a blank screen as I try to finish this chapter. Out of the dead silence, I suddenly hear a voice: "Hey, sleepy-head! Yeah, you."

I think I'm drinking too much coffee now for sure. It's amazing what the mind can do when exhausted.

"*Hey!* Down here!" Then I hear a shrill whistle!

I look down at my cards, and it seems like the Devil card is moving! He's waving an arm at me!

As I stare down at that card that's looking at me, the Devil says, "Do I have your attention now? You're awake, after all. I thought you were going to fall asleep right into your cup of coffee there."

I'm thinking, "This can't be happening," and then, as if reading my mind, he says, "Oh, yes it can, my friend. I figured it was about time you and I had a little chitchat," he says, with a grin.

Wow! I gasp, coughing out a cloud of cigarette smoke.

"Easy, friend, easy," he says. "You shouldn't be smoking those things, ya know. Bad for ya."

"What the hell do you care!" I blurt out to the card, and then I think, "What am I doing? I'm talking to a tarot card! I'd better get to bed."

"Well, they are bad for you—cigarettes, that is. And don't blame me for your bad habit. I had nothing to do with that," says the Devil as he pushes the ashtray toward me.

"But aren't you against all of mankind? My smoking should make you happy!"

"Actually I have nothing against mankind at all. I'm not a bad guy, once you get to know me. I'm a real angel, you know." He bats his eyes and gives me a big smile.

"Oh, the Devil is a comedian now too, huh? Well, don't quit your day job, pal," I say as I crush out the cigarette in the already-full ashtray.

"Well that's what gets my goat," he replies. "Excuse the pun. *Goat*— get it?" He winks. "I have been persecuted throughout the ages, and for what? Tell me one thing I did so bad to anyone."

"OK, how about tempting Jesus in the wilderness?" I say, leaning forward and pointing a finger right at him.

The Devil snaps back, "You're on, friend. Let me tell you how that all really went down—" he begins to say as he scratches his tail.

"And quit calling me *friend*!" I interrupt.

"Ooooh. Aren't we touchy today! OK, I'll call you …Vince? Is that good for you?"

"Yes, I guess my name is OK. As long as you don't get my soul or anything by saying my name. You don't, do you?"

"Oh, please! I'm not into souls".

"So what really happened in the wilderness, then?" I ask. "As if you're going to convince me of anything. Please go ahead and give it your best. This will be fun to hear you squirm out of."

"I bet you I can convince you my intentions were good ones," he replies as he stands up quickly, pointing a finger at me.

"*Ha!*" I howl back. I'm getting comfortable talking with this card. "What you wanna bet me? Oh, let me guess—my soul? Not a chance, friend.

"Drop the soul thing, will ya? I hear that so much. I have absolutely no desire for your soul. What am I gonna do with a soul, anyway—sell it on eBay?

Let's get this straight, Vince: I don't collect souls. That was put on me years ago, and not true at all. Only you can control your soul. More bum wrap. How about we wager just a handshake? Or are you afraid to shake my hand?"

"Hell no, I'm not afraid! Your just a tarot card! And I'm just imagining this whole thing anyway, so you got a bet!" as I reach out for his hand to shake.

We shake hands, and he smiles at me as he begins explaining the whole wilderness thing with Jesus.

"First off," the Devil starts, "I was just trying to help make the world a better place. As you can see from what it is now, I didn't succeed."

"*Ha!* The Devil trying to make the world a better place. I'm sure you'll be considered for the Nobel Peace Prize."

"OK, OK—look, the very first thing I offered Jesus was to turn stone into bread, right? Of course your *black book* calls it 'tempting,' not 'offering', but either way, that was the first thing I asked Jesus about, right?"

"Well, yes from what I remember, yes. And he told you 'Man does not live by bread alone'" I answer.

"That's right, that's what he said. But if he could turn stone into bread, he could have fed the masses! No more starvation! Isn't that a good thing? I thought it was, but nooooo. I was a bad angel for offering that."

"OK, OK. Maybe Jesus just didn't trust you—probably would have been stale bread, anyway."

"OK—how about the second offer I made him? I told him if he were to honor me, all the kingdoms of the world would be his."

"No, you told him to *bow down* before you, and all the kingdoms of the world would be his," I reply.

"OK, maybe I got a little dramatic there—but all the kingdoms of the world? Come on! I think a little respect might have been in order, even if he is the boss's son. And if he had all the kingdoms of the world, guess what that would mean?" he asks.

I answered back, looking blankly, "Wha—?"

Leaning toward me, and looking into my eyes, he says, "No more war! That's what! If you own everything, who are you gonna pick a fight with?"

"Well, you gotta point there ... I guess," I say to him, scratching my head.

"Thank you very much!" the Devil snaps back with a pompous grin.

"OK, continue on, Mr. D. What about the last temptation, or offer, as you put it?"

"Well, I suggested that Jesus cast himself from the high place we were standing on down to the rocks below, knowing that the angels would swoop down and snatch him up before he hit bottom."

"So what's that gonna prove?" I snap back.

"So what?" he says. "So what? Well, the people would have seen that great spectacular thing happening, right?"

"Yeah, I guess so."

"OK," he continues, "OK, here is why that would be a good thing. If the people saw the angels come out of the sky, swoop down, and catch Jesus before he hit the rocks and then place him back up on the high place, wouldn't that be better than the air show in Chicago!"

"Yes that would be something to see. So you just wanted a little entertainment, then?"

"No!" says the Devil. "If the people see, with their own eyes, the angels do such a fantastic thing like that for Jesus, then all would know that he was the true son of God. No more doubt. Everyone in the world would be Christian after that happened. No other religions, which means no bitterness between one religion and another. And no more war based on religion, either. All would be on the same page.

"So Vince, let's review this whole thing about the three temptations in the wilderness. OK—first turn stone into bread, which equals lots of bread to eat for starving people. Second, owning all the kingdoms of the world means peace on earth. No wars. Third, everyone would know beyond a doubt the Jesus was the true son of God, and there would be only one true religion to follow because of it.

"Now, don't you think the world might have been a better place if he had taken me up on my offers?"

"Well," I say to card number fifteen. "Maybe you did get a bum wrap. I'll try to keep that in mind when you come up in my readings, OK? Fair enough?"

"Fair enough," says the Devil.

"Oh, Mr. D., one more thing."

"Yes?" he answers.

"I'm almost out of cigarettes; can you turn this empty pack into a full pack for me?"

"Now, you're the comedian Vince. Don't you quit your day job!" With that, the card becomes still again—a frozen image, just as before this conversation, and I think to myself, "*Wow!* That was some visualization I just had! I better get to sleep. One more smoke, and then off to bed." As I go to shake out my last cigarette in the pack, I see the pack is full. It's a brand-new pack of smokes! Well, now—I guess I do owe the Devil!
Thanks, Mr. D., and goodnight.

Empress: Number 3
~ The Mother ~

"Good morning, Vin. Coffee?"

"Wha—? Looking at the clock, it said 6:00 a.m. I guess I should get up anyway.

"Coffee, Vin?"

"What? Who said *coffee?* Who's here? Only my mother calls me Vin. Ma?"

"Over here, sleepy head."

There was my tarot deck next to a cup of fresh coffee steaming away on the night stand. I stared at it, trying to wake up and figure out what the hell was going on here. As I gathered my thoughts, I noticed the top card of my deck was face up. It was the Empress, and she had a big smile on her face!

"Now you're awake," she said. "I made the coffee just like you like it. Only three scoops, and the rest of the pot is poured into your thermos on the counter. I washed your cup out too. It was filthy."

"Thought it looked different" I said, staring at the clean cup. What's on your mind?" I said as I grabbed my robe.

"You needed a visit," she sighed as she gently patted my forearm. "I noticed you're doing well, and I thought you needed to be reminded of that."

"I am?".

"Yes, you are doing exactly as you wanted to do. You have most every-thing you sought to get out of life, Vin."

"I do, huh? Well, where the hell is it all, then?"

"Look around you, Vin. What are the things you want? What are the things you have? Anything missing?"

"I can use some things," I said as I looked around the room.

"Yes everyone can use some more 'things,' but do they need them, and at what price do you pay to acquire those things anyway? You have to scurry around hustling to be at places you don't want to be, doing things you don't want to do. That's the price you pay for those things' you think you can use. Is it worth it? What are your plans for today, Vin?"

"I don't really know yet." I yawned, with the coffee waiting at my mouth for the chance to enter. "Probably some phone readings and work on my book some, A few clients at the coffee house this afternoon."

"Oooh, poor deprived boy you are. Ooooh. You pay your bills every month, you have food in the fridge, a few dollars in your wallet, a car, and a phone. What are you missing? You have your health, even though I wish you would quit smoking those darn cigarettes. Not to mention the drinking."

"I bought a pipe, and I'm cutting down. I don't know; I just feel like I should have more. Most people do at my age, ya know."

"Most people at your age don't have something you do have that is golden."

"Oh, and what's that?" I asked.

"Happiness. They are controlled and manipulated, and their time is not theirs. Yes, they have money in the bank that they probably will never use. They have a shiny new car, a big house with a manicured lawn, nice expensive furniture that they try not to scratch, and nice new clothes that don't feel any more comfortable than your old clothes feel. Don't you see what you acquired? The ability not to need and still be happy and feel secure. You live a life without luxury and riches, but you're happy. You might not realize it, but you feel more secure than a lot of the people who have all that other stuff, including money in the bank. It's funny, but the more people have, the less secure they feel. Drink your coffee, it's getting cold."

"OK, I'm drinking it."

"Your livelihood is a card reader. That's a big accomplishment."

"It is? Well, where's all the money, if it's such a big accomplishment?"

"Who said anything about money? You're confusing money with actual wealth.

"There is no established system to do what you do—no unions or ads in the paper saying, 'tarot reader wanted.' Isn't that what you always wanted? To be a reader and not part of the system? You always hated the system anyway. Nine to five and all that. But that is the game most people want to play. Bless them, and hope that they are happy. They did what they wanted, and you have too. You are rich in your own way, Vin. You have all the things you wanted to have, and you stopped spending time trying to get things you thought you were supposed to want, things you didn't really want but felt you were expected to try to get: married with children, house in the 'burbs, full-time job, traffic jams, church on Sunday morning, BBQ on weekends, and watching the game on TV after you cut the grass. That is not you, Vin! Yes, you tried it. You didn't like it, so you took a different path. Your own path. And your path was reading tarot cards.

"How many decks do you have in here right now" she said as she looked around the room.

I noticed the deck on the shelf and one on my desk. "Two decks," I said.

"Ahah," she said. "What about in that black box over there?"

"Oh yeah, two more decks in there too."

"And how about this deck here on the shelf?"

"Oh, yeah, forgot that one."

"So—five decks of tarot cards in a one-room studio apartment."

"Well, to be honest, I have about ten more decks in that big trunk there that I use as a coffee table."

"Where else do you have them, Vin? Fess up."

"Well, I'm not hiding them, for cryin' out loud! Jeez, you're acting like my mother now."

"Well, I am the Empress, and I do live in every mother, so that would make sense. Where else? Come on, now."

"OK, let's see: one deck in my jeep. No, two decks in my jeep. Lynda's kitchen, top of the fridge. Hell, I don't exactly know how many decks I have hanging around here! A lot of them."

"And you use them too, don't you?"

"Yes, I use them. That's my bread and butter."

"Exactly!" she said as she poured me more coffee. "So you see, you're successful.

You want me to make you some waffles?"

What? No ma'am, I mean Empress," I said as I lit another cigarette. "Waffles! Ha!"

"You should eat."

"I know." I nodded. "I want to tell you that I appreciate you reminding me of where I'm at and how I'm doing. It helps, and I guess we should all stop and count our blessings from time to time. But right now I have to get changed and run some errands."

"Not before you finish your waffles. They're on the counter in the kitchen."

"But I don't want any waffles!"

"Eat your waffles, ... and don't slouch!

"I'm not eating waffles — like I said, I got things to do. What you gonna do about it? Ground me? Ha!"

"Well, good luck finding your car keys till that plate is clean."

"Hey! What'd you do with my keys!"

"Have a good day, son. I'll check in on you later."

"Yeah, that's what I'm afraid of!" I said with a mouthful of waffles. "Ya know what! This talk with you is scarier than the talk I had with that Devil card!"

Justice: Number 11
~ Words ~

As I sat at my desk looking over the things I wanted to cover in my book, I heard someone clear their throat. But there's no one here but me. Then I heard a loud banging like metal on stone! It echoed through my small apartment! Wow! Someone has a broken water pipe? That's when a set of scales was thrown in front of me! *Crash!* I looked down at the scales, and they were right next to the Justice card. And there she was, the lady of Justice leaning over in her throne, looking right at me.

"Court's in session!" she blared out.

I looked twice and blinked my eyes, but she didn't go away. "Hello," I said, acknowledging her presence.

"Well, here you are, putting words into your book."

"Yes, that's true," I said. "Words come in handy when writing a book, wouldn't you agree?"

"Well, words have their place, yes," she answered back as she casually picked off some lint from her gown. "But they are overrated, you know," she said, sitting with those deep eyes staring right through me.

"How so?" I asked.

Then she leaned forward and said, "Did you know that ninety-three percent of what we communicate to others is nonverbal? That is to say, only seven percent of how we communicate with others is through words. Still think words mean a lot? Your intent is going into that book more than the words are.

"The real justice system can't be debated or denied. True justice is based on universal principles—not on words. Your US Constitution and your Declaration of Independence represent truth. But how those words are perceived depends on the individual.

"You have nine Supreme Court Justices who read the same words called your US Constitution who cannot unanimously agree on what those words say. Real justice is truth and has no book of laws to interpret. It just is, and that's that. Authority isn't always truth. Truth is authority.

"In your country you have the right to life, liberty, and the pursuit of happiness. That's cute. You also have the right to death. For without death, you have no life. Justice is based on duality in your world: Good and evil. Right and wrong. Mankind puts one against the other and tries to interpret which is which. Muslim, Jew. Black, white. Gay, straight. Republican, Democrat. No one focuses on truth. They're too busy hating and fearing the other side. Going through life with blinders on."

"Wow," I said, striking a match to light a cigarette and wondering where this was all going.

Justice looked at me with a smile and continued. "If the whole world was only good, and there wasn't any evil, you would never know what good is. It would just be the norm. The same holds true with love. If you loved everyone, you would never know that love ever existed. In your world, you cannot understand or perceive anything if it has no duality to it. This is why God is such a puzzle to mankind. God has no duality.

"Know this, Vincent: nothing exist except God. There is no 'outside' of God. God has no edges to it. God is in everything. Which means it's OK to feel you are a part of God. But the physical plain is all dualities: Space and matter. Time, life, death, love, fear, happiness, and sorrow. What you really are is a part of this universe you call God. You are immeasurably old and have taken on millions of different shapes and forms and the coming and going of those shapes and forms are just a universal pulse of an eternal *one*: God.

"You are the universe witnessing and experiencing itself from billions of different points of view. Each one of you is a point of view. And the coming and going of these points of view keeps things moving along—evolving and changing all the time for a different look. This way the feeling of what you really are is constantly changing. That keeps things interesting, doesn't it?"

"Wow. Sounds kinda scary, actually," I said.

"Oh? So change scares you? Why? Because it is the unknown. That's why. Don't be such a candy-ass," she shot back, pointing that big sword toward me.

"Hey! Don't get so touchy. I'm just trying to understand!" I snapped. "You're talking words, universe, and god and all this stuff; I'm just trying to write a book."

"Ah, don't take it so personal," she replied. "It's supposed to be a little scary. If it wasn't challenging, it would be kinda boring around here, wouldn't it? So it's sorta like a roller coaster ride for approximately seventy or eighty years," she explained as she waved her sword tip up and down.

"That's a long time!" I said.

"Is it?" she replied. "You have nothing but time. You are eternal. You're part of the most perfect thing there is. You are a part of the universe. You have nothing to gain. What can you possibly gain when you already are *everything* to begin with," she said as she looked into my eyes. The real law of justice is this: When you enter this physical plane, you forget who and what you really are. Which is eternal perfection. Otherwise, being here while knowing you were eternal would just be soooo boring."

"I'm trying to evolve myself. Become enlightened. Be better than what I am all the time, but sometimes it's not easy," I replied.

"Enlightenment? You come down here into this physical arena limited to just five senses for a short time because it is challenging. It is enriching. So live the physical plane. Experience it," she said.

"Why is it necessary if I'm perfect already?" I said.

"It's not necessary," she replied. "It's enriching. Dancing isn't necessary, but the soul likes it. Painting a picture or being inspired in some way isn't necessary, but these things feed the soul. They are like addictions! And that is what you do here. It's good for you to experience the physical."

"Addictions! I have the Justice card telling me addictions are good!" I said.

"You're born with addictions," she responded. "You are addicted to breathing, sleeping, eating, water, sex. Don't those things feel exhilarating when you want them and you get them? You are here to experience the physical plane. Which means you cannot survive without addictions."

Then she continued to say, "I get a real kick out of people who think they are supposed to deprive themselves of addiction to become more enlightened. Fasting on a mountaintop somewhere like a lump on a log.

That's exactly what they came from! Perfection. And that's exactly what they will be going back to. Perfection. So why come here to be exactly what you are to begin with? The reason you come here is to experience the physical. Not ignore it. To experience imperfection and challenge.

"Your religions that use the Bible as law have been contorted and twisted with words of confusion and contradiction. The Old Testament is based on "laws and judgment", but the New Testament is based on "love and grace". An eye for an eye, or turn the other cheek. Words. Take a closer look at your Bible. You will find all sorts of real life in it. Jesus wasn't religious; Jesus never said, 'The Kingdom of God is like a church service that goes on and on forever and never ends.' He said the kingdom was like a homecoming celebration, a wedding, a party, a feast to which all are invited. Like that song 'Cabaret': 'Come taste the wine, come hear the band, come blow your horn, start celebrating, right this way your table's waiting!' Gosh! I love Liza! But seriously, enjoy your time here. Don't focus on what you feel are your faults. You are experiencing being mortal.

And that is a real change from what you really are. Immortal. Immortal and perfect."

I just stared like a deer caught in the headlights as she continued.

"As long as you live and let live, you are doing just fine being mortal. Love who you are, and accept your weaknesses, but have fun wrestling with them too. And remember, you are perfection. That is truth." With that, she picked up her scales from my floor and froze back into the card.

"Hey!" I called out. "You got sand all over my carpet!"

"So sue me," she replied as she faded off.

Death: Number 13
~ The Unknown ~

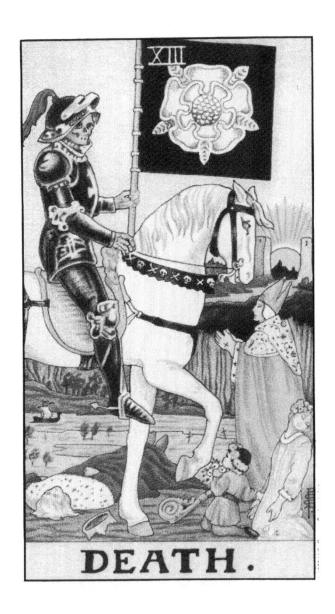

Sitting at my computer, working on the last chapter of my book, I glanced at my deck of tarot cards. The Death card appeared to be looking right at me.

I needed to take a break. Midnight already! As I rise and turn from my chair, I walk right into card number thirteen standing tall and still. Death!

"Uh! Aren't you a little early!" I said in a total shock.

"That's what most people say when I drop by," he answered.

Hoping to get on his good side, I said, "Uh, well, hello, Mr. Death card, uh. How are you? Uh, you look real good for yourself. Been working out? I wasn't expecting to see you so soon. Uh, I'm gonna be sixty, or I was."

"Ah. Don't get all excited; I'm not here for that. It's not your time yet."

"*Whew!* Thank God." I gasped, resting my forehead in both hands.

"Just heard you were writing about a few of the cards, so I thought I would drop by. I mean, I'm a pretty big name in the tarot, wouldn't you agree?" He said as he scraped a bony finger over the edge of that sickle.

"Yeah, big, but not too welcome," I replied.

"That's what I mean. I wanted to get that straightened out. I think I'm being misrepresented. I mean, come on now. It's not all that dramatic."

What: *dying?*" I shouted.

"Yes. Dying. You all must die at some time. So what's the problem? Why don't you just accept that simple and inevitable fact? It's a transition, that's all."

"A transition to what?" I asked.

"I could tell you – but then I'd have to kill you." he answered.

"Oh, now Death is a comedian," I said, rolling my eyes.

"But really, telling you would take all the fun out of living. People get too bent out of shape over dying. But the more you accept death as a reality of life, the more you live your life while here. It's a natural process. People that know I'm coming soon will tell you that.

They live each day and hour with eyes wide open, loving every minute. They become more alive. They realize how beautiful this wonderful gift of life is. Everyone else is busy thinking about trivial nonsense. People don't realize the impact they could have while here. Life is a play, and each of you are the leading role. Your performance can be good, or it can be lousy. Either way, at the end, you are going to say, 'So, how did I do?' Will others applaud your performance when it's over, or will they just walk away thinking it was no big deal? This is your time to shine. Put your heart into your life. Savor every minute. And make a difference. Leave with a standing ovation!"

"Wow, that was really a good sales pitch," I said. "But it still doesn't make you a welcomed sight. Sorry, but nooo thanks."

"Still afraid of dying? Why?"

"Because I don't know what happens afterward. That's why."

"It's not for me to tell you what happens after you leave here, but ask yourself this: What's the worst that could happen? *Nothing*. That's the worst that could happen. Nothing. You just go to sleep and never wake up again. Just nothing," he snapped back. "But if there is something more afterward, you're in like Flynn. Correct?"

I just stared with a blank expression at the skeletal figure before me.

"You still don't get it, do you?" he asked.

"I can't die yet. I'm writing a book," I said.

"Ah, don't worry about that. I'm not going to be back until after your book is finished."

"OK, then I'll take my time to finish it. Maybe another forty years!

"So you want to live to be a hundred, then?"

"I don't know," I said. "I guess, yeah."

"Really? Have you ever visited a nursing home Vince? See those lucky one-hundred-year-old souls. Tell me if you feel they're happy. Their bodies still work, but it becomes difficult for the spirit to stay strong."

"I tell you what, Death. You're a real depressing pain in the ass, you know that? I was having a real good day until your bony ass came by."

"See ya soon, Vince."

"Yeah, that's what I'm afraid of. So take your time. Put me at the bottom of your to-do list, OK?"

"Finish your book, Vince."

"It's gonna take a looooong time to finish. It's a twenty-eight-volume encyclopedia set on dental floss."

"I know it's a book on the tarot, Vince."

"Hey, Death, I gotta skeleton joke for you: a skeleton walks into a bar and orders a beer .... and a mop. Get it?

"Clock's ticking, Vince."

"OK, OK. Hey, really. I'm not going to be wearing no marble hat anytime soon, am I?"

"Tick tock, tick tock."

"Ya know what? You should get some Neosporin. Might help clear up that bony skeletal condition and improve your appearance."

"Vince, someday you will look just like me. And quit smoking those cigarettes. I don't plan on being back here for a while, and I'd hate to make a special trip."

With that, he froze back into the card.

The High Priestess Number 2
~ Mystery ~

I sat at my desk ready to write. The room was silent except for the ticking of the clock. The candle fluttered in the dimly lit room and the smoke of incense sorta danced with the flame. I started my chapter on the High Priestess, and just the thought of that card made me wonder about much: the mysterious High Priestess. As I looked at that card, I thought that she is one of the most popular cards in the tarot, for sure. Yes, queen of the hop!

Then I heard a voice say, "Thank you."

What? Who said *Thank you?*

Then I heard it again: "Thank you."

I looked at my deck and there on the top was the High Priestess with a smile coming across her face. She was beautiful sitting there dressed in her flowing, blue gown and wearing that crescent-moon headdress.

"Wow!" I said as I gave a blank stare at the card addressing me. "I never expected you to come forth. Other cards, maybe yes, but you! The High Priestess? I'm honored. Please excuse the mess." I tried in vain to straighten up my desk area.

"You don't have to make such a fuss," she said. "I know much about you. More than you realize. More than you know about yourself." She smirked.

"Oh. Well, yes, I guess you would. It's just I didn't take a shower yet or shave or nothin', and I would have if I knew you were going to visit me." I tried to straighten my hair out a little bit and sit straighter as I adjusted my chair.

"Oh, nonsense!" she said as she waved her hand in the air as if to swipe my words away. "So, what are you going to write about me?"

"Well, I'm not sure yet. I was going to sit here and just see what comes to me. You know, sorta intuitive-like. That's what you're all about, anyway, so I figured that would be a good approach. You know, being the High Priestess and all."

"Good idea," she said as she leaned forward, looking into my computer screen. "Just let things flow, I always say."

"I think you are gonna be the hardest for me to write about, though. I always sorta favored you over the others," I said, trying not to sound too silly.

"Well, I'm flattered. So you think of me how, then?" She smiled as she gave me a flirtatious glance. "Unattainable? Mysterious? After all, I am the virgin," she said with a smile.

"I'm not sure why I feel that way about you, actually, but I do. Never cared about the virgin thing, really. You're just special."

"Oh, yes you do, my dear. You see, the fact that I am mysterious is what makes you feel that way. The unattainable High Priestess makes you want to attain me all the more. But if you did attain me, then that power would be destroyed for ever. My essence is mystery. Once mystery is known, it is no longer a mystery. That's the paradox of it. I am mystery. So you see, in order for me to exist, you must never attain me in any way, shape, or form. For, once you do, my essence will be gone."

"So the virgin things stands for more than just a sexual energy?" I said.

"Sure it does, Vincent. It stands for the mystery and wonder of things. The unknown. That has a real power in itself, mystery does. Although mankind has really exploited the sexual thing to an extreme. And let's not forget getting tossed into a volcano every now and then."

"How so? The sexual thing, I mean."

"'How?' you say? Man has always been fascinated with all the sexuality of woman. Women give birth, women have breasts, women have menstrual cycles. Women have multiple orgasms! Let's face it: women have a lot more sexual vibration than men do. And if men cannot have or experience all of that sexuality, then the next best thing is to own it. And men have owned women for centuries."

"I agree." I said "But that is changing now. Don't you think?"

"About time, wouldn't you say?" she answered.

"So let me get this straight. If I want you in some manner in my life, and I get that, then I destroy the very thing I wanted about you. Therefore, the only way to keep your essence is to leave you alone?"

"You got it. So here I sit," she said.

"Any regrets?" I gave her a curious look.

"You'll never know," she said.

"Gee, I really think you're something. Can I call you sometime?"

"You know where to find me," she answered as I heard her voice drift away.

"Hey! Wait a minute! Hey! I think I'm in love! No, really! Don't go yet! Damn—I'm in love with a damn tarot card!

"That's it! Oh well, story of my life. Always looking for my soul mate, and she's always just out of reach. Time to get to bed." I crushed out my smoke and finished the last of my glass of wine, got in bed, and turned off the light.

As I lay there, dozing in and out of sleep, I felt a gentle breeze around my face, followed by the wisp of fine cloth brushing against my cheek. As I realized this experience to be more than a dream, a soft hand touched my cheek, and then the soft voice of that mystery woman whispered into my ear: "I will always be here in your heart."

Then I felt a kiss on my cheek. "I am everywhere and in a thousand faces. Your book might take some aspects of mystery out of the tarot, which means it takes some mystery out of me." was the last thing I remembered hearing before drifting off into sleep.

ABOUT THE AUTHOR

Vincent Pitisci's client base is worldwide from servicemen in Afghanistan to men and women throughout the U.S. He also teaches and lectures on the Tarot in Wisconsin and Illinois. Pitisci's private practice and residence is in Chicago's southwest suburb of Berwyn, IL.

More information on Vincent can be found on his website - www.pitisci.com